16
SECONDS

Debunking The Myths
Surrounding Manifestation

PAM LIDFORD

AND

SANDRA STOCKS

16 Seconds

First published in 2021 by

Panoma Press Ltd
48 St Vincent Drive, St Albans, Herts, AL1 5SJ, UK
info@panomapress.com
www.panomapress.com

Book layout by Neil Coe.

978-1-784529-34-5

The right of Pam Lidford and Sandra Stocks to be identified as the authors of this work has been asserted in accordance with sections 77 and 78 of the Copyright, Designs and Patents Act 1988.

A CIP catalogue record for this book is available from the British Library.

This book is available online and in bookstores.

Dedication

We dedicate this with love to all the beautiful souls
who are ready to wake up energetically and live the
life they came here to live.

Endorsements

"Energy is the missing link and why most people are frustrated with spiritual development. *16 Seconds – Debunking The Myths Surrounding Manifestation* recognises that there are more layers to creating your reality than just goal setting or knowing about the Law of Attraction. This book unusually combines how our brain can either support or sabotage us, together with a much deeper understanding of what we attract at a vibrational level. Using tools, techniques and sharing their personal stories, Pam and Sandra's knowledge, different approaches and deep understanding of the subject shines through to guide us to our own awareness of how we think and feel and how we can shape our light bulb moments to attract what we *do* want and away from what we *don't* want."

Christy Whitman, *New York Times* bestselling Author and Master Certified Coach

"This is a book that clearly helps the reader to realise how we *truly and fundamentally* create our reality using the principles of the vibrational Law of Attraction together with an understanding of how our brain can either support or sabotage our efforts. The tools and personal stories shared in this book makes it a must read for anyone who is ready to manifest a more empowered and fulfilled life. Included are a number of practical exercises to support the theories, and Sandra and Pam obviously come from a point of experience. Highly recommended to those who wish to make positive changes in their life!"

Henriette Maasdijk, Founder, Vibrational Healing Foundation

Acknowledgements - Pam

There are so many wonderful people who have helped me get to where I am today in the form of family, friends, teachers and mentors along with my beautiful clients who I have coached, as well as those I have been privileged to train to become coaches.

The Coaching Academy set me on the path to becoming a professional coach and I thank them for it. Carmel Hayes, who encouraged me to go into teaching in 1993 which started my love of sharing information. Luli Harvey who let me bring life coaching and personal development into education. David Bowker, a wonderful boss (who is missed). Steve Lidford who believed in me, let me practise on him and supported me in every way imaginable in the early days. Chris Milbank who taught me Thought Field Therapy, Reflective Repatterning and so many other cutting edge tools way ahead of them becoming popular. Jane Foster, my dear friend who brought coaching to my attention in 2002 (you are missed). My daughter Rebecca, who let me practise everything I learned, both then and now, on her. Peter Goodman for reading our chapters and checking the contracts, and of course, the lovely Sandra Stocks who encouraged me to write this book with her, a beautiful soul and cherished friend.

Acknowledgements - Sandra

There are many wonderful friends, teachers, mentors and clients who have been an integral part of this incredible voyage called Life, and who have guided and supported me in my learning and given me the encouragement to turn my passion to help people into my absolute purpose and into this book. There are far too many people to list individually and I thank you all with much love, but I want to give a special thank you to the wonderful first readers of this book, including my Patia, Sharmaine Rainsbury and especially my girls, Holly and her partner Ellie, who went through it with a lovingly critical fine-toothed comb! Liz Trubridge who opened my eyes to the beauty and power of crystals – what a journey we've been on! Thank you to Henriette Maasdijk who has always and still does inspire me with her knowledge of all things vibrational.

I want to express huge gratitude to The Coaching Academy for teaching me the framework from which I work. A big shout out, with huge love and appreciation, for Christy Whitman, my coach – a pioneer in vibrational coaching and an absolute inspiration to me. Thank you Christy for your love and encouragement. Not forgetting my online mentors and the daily presence of Abraham – thank you Esther Hicks.

I thank Martin, my blessing of a husband who supports me unwaveringly in all I do and my children Holly, Jessica and Harry – where would I be without you? And to Moira, my sister, who has always been in my corner – thank you for co-creating the relationship we now have. And of course, to my dear friend Pam Lidford, who agreed to come on this fun trip with me to pour our learnings on to these pages to inspire and transform people's lives. Thank you! It's been a ride!

Not forgetting you, our reader. It is because of you that I gained the inspiration to write this book.

And lastly, huge appreciation for my Higher Self, always having my back and continually guiding me back to my purpose.

Contents

Introduction

"If you wish to understand the Universe, think of energy, frequency and vibration."

– Nikola Tesla

Sandra

As a young six-year-old girl, I knew that there was more 'out there' than what I could see, hear, feel, touch and smell. I wasn't quite sure what that meant, but looking back I now know it was the 'more' that I was fascinated with. The limitlessness, the intangible, the 'something that I couldn't quite put my finger on'. And as I got older, this seemed to fade into the background as I lived my life, not having any idea how to *create* my life.

I lived a life that was, for the most part, conditional. As long as those around me were happy, then it meant that everything was OK. And if you're doing that too, you'll know that it doesn't work out too well for you. So I lived a life of mediocrity – some highs, quite a few lows, until in my late 30s I was told my mum was going to die in seven weeks from terminal cancer and my dad followed within a year. Once the shock of becoming an orphan finally started to fade and grief set in, I started to feel very old questions start to surface, such as 'There must be more?' 'Is this it?' And then after the quick loss of both my parents, the question 'Life's too short – there must be another way to live?'

What I now know to my absolute core is that the question I was really asking was *'Life's too short – there must be another way to **create*** *the life that I want to live?*' And that question led me on my journey of understanding that within every individual is both the physical (ego) which is our flesh and bones, thoughts and beliefs and the non-physical (spiritual) which is ever-present, all-knowing, abundant, loving and connected to all that there is within the universal expanse of energy. Both play a part in the life we create.

My desire to create a life that felt right *for me* has led to many years of study, research, supporting others with transformation and having fun while learning to trust in the benevolent energies that surround us in this awe-inspiring Universe.

I have used my knowledge and guided (thank you Higher Self) wisdom to bring awareness to thousands of people of how energy, thoughts, emotions and beliefs can either create a life you do want or will create a life that you don't want, leading to frustration that you're not experiencing the life you truly desire even though you think you're doing all the right things! And that's where the magic of this book lies.

Pam and I have come together to bring you a book that explains how you are currently creating the life you are living, through the vibrational energy you are emitting and the brain's insistence that it keeps you safe and thereby looks to sabotage any move you make to break out of your comfort zone and move into something new. It's a passion of ours to support people to identify and release habits, patterns, beliefs, thoughts and perspectives that keep you limited and shift them so that you can know yourself and your life in your true state – unlimited.

We have dedicated this book to all who truly want to understand how to fully implement the workings of the Law of Attraction (together with the other supportive universal laws) and therefore debunk the myths that confuse and stop you using them for your benefit. We also want you to know how beliefs are formed and how the brain develops those beliefs, how they hold vibration, and depending on how your thoughts think, will indicate their energetic magnetism resulting in what they will attract and manifest. And all of this takes place within 16 seconds…

In our book, we have shared personal stories, research, and most importantly, ways and tools to change any limiting thoughts into empowering vibrational beliefs that will then result in you being a match, both in your thought and vibration, to what you want. We show you how to become aware of your emotions, which are guiding you either away from your desires or closer to where you want to get to. We also debunk the familiar myths out there relating to the Law of Attraction and instead, support you with suggestions to follow through on, bringing you into harmony with the accurate and omnipresent universal laws. And finally, how awareness is key within the first 16 seconds, when the vibration of your emotion is picked up by the Law of Attraction and brings you more of what you are feeling and thinking and therefore attracting.

Our wish for you is that by the end of this book you will know what you didn't know so you can know what you need to know to attract what you want and create the reality that *you* desire.

Happy manifesting!

With much love, Sandra xx

Pam

Books offer the reader an opportunity to indulge in an interesting story, learn something new and/or disagree with what they are reading; whichever way you look at it, they create an energy and emotion within us.

I've loved reading and learning new things for as long as I can remember; as a child I enjoyed reading both fact and fantasy, the thought of escaping into a new story made me happy and I looked forward to it. Finding out something new about life through history or English excited me. I love books. I love the feel of them, the look of them and the weight in my hand.

So having spent over 35 years within the personal development industry, initially personally to help me understand myself better, and later professionally for over 25 years working alongside others who wanted to understand themselves better, in the role of teacher, coach, public speaker and trainer, when Sandra asked me if I'd be interested in writing a book together about how to manifest more of what makes us feel good, I said yes.

For over 25 years I've been privileged to be in a position to be able to share lots of practical personal development tips along with mental and emotional health techniques with audiences around the UK and occasionally abroad, pretty much on a weekly basis, delivered in training rooms and via Zoom with adult learners. I love sharing in this way, but I wanted to reach more people so they could discover just how much choice they **can** have over their life, when they gain awareness of what's causing them to manifest what they don't want and how to change it by debunking the myths around the Law of Attraction.

Though I love coaching and it's changed my life for the better, over the years I've chosen to be trained in many different fields, which I've added into my holistic practice. Often, I trained because I wanted to help myself 'heal' or recover from past emotional experiences; sometimes I trained just because it sounded interesting and along the way I discovered simple techniques, which when used regularly, give you control over manifesting the life you want.

I've practised everything I bring you in my chapters. Some exercises were more suited to my character than others so worked faster. Sandra and I wanted to bring you many to try via the playsheets in the separate download www.playsheets.16seconds.co.uk so you could choose the ones that might work best for your preferences, as there isn't a one size fits all.

Life can be a mixed bag, sometimes it's wonderful, other times very challenging and that's life. But I've discovered it's how we handle challenges that counts and it's attitude, mindset and resilience that make the difference between falling into a state of disempowerment or victim mentality or rising up to a state of flow, learning and growth.

My life isn't perfect, but it is wonderful and I'm so glad I let go of striving for 'perfect' many years ago. Perfectionism can cause procrastination because when we're so fearful of failing, we struggle to complete things in case they aren't 100% right. But failure is a gift, it offers us an opportunity to learn so we can do something different when we next try.

So when I understood this I decided to 'try' to learn from my mistakes and do something different next time, whether that was behaving differently, feeling a different emotion or taking a different action. It took time, but awareness is such a wonderful thing to have as it gives you choice as well as the opportunity to manifest more of what you want.

For me it's important to acknowledge how I feel about an experience or event, be it positive or negative, so I can be honest with myself, move through it, release it and no matter how challenging the event was, to find the lesson from it so I can make the best of the experience and move on. The alternative is being trapped or owned by the negative emotion which brings you more of what you don't want.

I'm so grateful to have met so many wonderful teachers along the way who appeared at just the right time, and helped me to learn how to help myself and start living an easier and more joyful life, and part of writing this book is to share some of those learnings with you.

My discoveries took me on a joyful journey of learning that included training in Energy Psychology, conventional psychology, coaching skills, mindfulness, the Law of Attraction and Neuro Linguistic Programming and I have also discovered a newly found interest in quantum physics and neuroscience coaching.

After working with thousands of people I've discovered that a little bit of one discipline blended with a little bit of another can create the magic needed to help make change happen and I wanted to share this idea with a larger audience, in my way, rather than within the confines of an agreed training course, and I'm excited to be able to do that here.

I trust you will find techniques within that will prove useful and interesting, and if you will consider focusing on them for

16 seconds… they may even start to change the results you get in your life.

Happy reading.

With love, Pam x

CHAPTER 1

Seven Universal Laws

Sandra

As Pam and I have written in our introduction to this book, everything that we are and everything that is around us and everything that we manifest is firstly energy. Everything that you see, think and feel starts as a vibration. And therefore, there is a relationship between the *energy* of our thoughts and emotions and what we are *physically* receiving. Understanding that premise is hugely empowering and beneficial to us all as we can then deliberately choose to think and feel thoughts that will energetically be a match to what we desire and as a result, what we then receive.

If you want to live the life that you planned to create when you first came on to this planet before we adopted contradictory thoughts, beliefs and behaviour patterns from those around us, it is important to be aware of some of the universal laws that are all tied together and govern how and what we create and manifest. There are many universal laws, however the laws I have mentioned here have a direct bearing on understanding your part in creating the life you want. Although the Law of Attraction will be referred to throughout this book, to have an understanding of these additional laws will help you to grasp the potential of deliberate creation.

1. The Law of Attraction

It seems that most people have now heard of this law that pervades everything in our Universe. The law that affects literally everything we create in our lives. But do we actually understand how this law works? Do we understand that we have complete control over what we create by what we think, say, act and feel thanks to the Law of Attraction bringing us more of what we're focusing and building momentum on, whether we want it or not?

This is something that is worth taking note of. The Law of Attraction is always fair, always consistent, and never wavers in its vibrational ability to bring you more of what you are focusing on and therefore creating. It is constantly working – it is an energy that is around and vibrating at all times and responding to the energy signals which we, as beacons, are putting out. It is as constant as the Law of Gravity.

Imagine yourself as a lighthouse beacon or as an energy tower, and with every thought you think and therefore with every emotion you feel, you are emitting a signal that the Law of Attraction picks up on and then sets into motion more thoughts or feelings or situations that match the signals that you are sending out. The Law of Attraction doesn't go into deciphering mode, such as 'Does she really mean that?' 'Is he sure that's what he wants?' It just consistently matches your vibrational signal and brings more like it, and the process begins within 16 seconds, depending on the strength of your signal.

The all-inclusive Law of Attraction

So, just think for a minute of how easily we repeat experiences that we don't give much conscious attention to, such as having a situation going on that we're not particularly happy with. It could be something that's happened when we're driving, or an argument with a friend or loved one, or an unhappy encounter with a sales assistant, and what do we tend to do? We unwittingly talk about it to anyone and everyone. We want our friends and loved ones to listen to us and even agree with us. We tweet it, we Facebook it. We may even post it on Instagram and although we feel we are *just* expressing how we feel, we have in fact by the attention we have given it upped the emotional energy focus of that particular situation, and by the momentum that we have now built, we are emitting a much stronger signal about the unhappy situation. And as the Law of Attraction is consistently fair, it will bring more like it into your experience, as I've already said, pretty quickly.

When I say more like it, this could be another thought to match it, more feelings to match the emotion you have about it and more situations like the one you have just lived. You are having that experience where you feel unfairly that 'stuff' just keeps happening to you. Until you change your vibrational focus about a topic, until you shift the way you think and feel about the topic, you will continue to attract the same. It may be different places, different faces but it will be the same occurrence. Let me give you a very clear example of how this happened to me personally before I really understood how this law works.

It was almost 20 years ago and it was December (I remember this clearly because Christmas was around the corner) and I was aware that my car insurance was up for renewal the following month, in January. I was very happy because I had one month to go and it looked like my no-claims bonus was going to increase and therefore the cost of my car insurance was going to decrease. So, I started to say to myself pretty regularly when I was in the car, 'don't have an accident', 'don't have an accident' and focusing on that intent. I was then asked to cover a meeting for the weight loss club for which I was a leader, which was out of my area and to which I agreed. I didn't know the exact location of this meeting so I drove through the rain and rush hour traffic, looking around to see if I could locate the particular road that would lead me to where I needed to be. As I did that, I didn't realise that the cars in front of me had pulled to a stop at a traffic light and yes, you've guessed it, I hit the back of the car in front of me and due to the accident being my fault, I lost my no-claims bonus.

Now you could say, but you were focusing on *not* having an accident so why did the Law of Attraction bring you an accident? And the very important reason is, **the Law of Attraction is inclusive, not exclusive**. It will bring you what you focus on whether you want it or not, so although I was *saying* 'don't have an accident', *my focus* was on the idea of an accident, and with my repetitive thoughts and words and my overriding emotion of concern about losing my no-claims bonus, I had built up a very strong momentum of that focus and became a vibrational match to the very thing I didn't want and the Law of Attraction responded in kind.

But the most wonderful realisation of this is that *we* are creating our reality every day, usually by default, but we can choose to *deliberately* create a life we truly want by giving attention to what feels good. And as I've just affirmed, the Law of Attraction is always fair, so the more you focus on feeling good (emotions such as love, appreciation, satisfaction of where you are right now, just to name a few), more of that will be drawn to you and your life will just get better and better. The drawback here as humans, living in this physical world, is that we give far more attention to what feels bad than what feels good and to switch this around, you have to give up being a lazy focuser and decide to milk the good feeling thoughts for all they're worth! And the pay off? You attract more of the good and let the energy vibration of the negative disappear out of your awareness.

Are you a lazy focuser?

But, at risk of repetition – however hugely important for the purpose of clarity – it is crucial to note that everything stems from our point of focus (emotional *and* thought focus as what you feel stems from what you think); whether that is a deliberate point of focus or the unconscious focus, which happens through habit, routine and repetition. Our patterns of thought and behaviour tend to be habitual, whether that's a morning routine, taking the same route to work, the same response to a certain trigger, a continued critical thought of what we may look like. And we won't even be aware that we are thinking or behaving in any particular way, it will just be the way we do what we do or think what we think. We think about what's going on around us without any awareness of where these formed habits are leading us.

But whether good or bad habits of thoughts or behaviour, useful or damaging, the Law of Attraction is bringing you more like it

– more thoughts to add to the thoughts you're already thinking leading to more of the same emotion you feel and more situations to which you create the same responses, building the momentum along the way. So right now, if you're not aware of the Law of Attraction and how it works, it is likely you are creating by default. You are just receiving more of what you are habitually feeling, thinking and doing, good or bad.

So imagine what we *can* create within our own reality by being aware of where our focus is in relation to our thoughts, beliefs and emotions around what we want to be, do or have. Are they moving us towards or away from what we desire? Our beliefs are crucial when it comes to creating our reality hand in hand with the Law of Attraction and we go into this in much more detail later in the book.

But how wonderful would it be to become a deliberate creator? One who has **pure** desire? A desire that is free of doubt, fear, worry and anxiety. A creator who is aware of what they are thinking, doing and *feeling* in this process of creating through vibrational focus. A creator who is consciously able to pivot in the moment of not feeling good and start to deliberately shift their focus on to a thought or behaviour that feels better, and start to build that moving forward momentum to what it is you want to be, do or have. To have the awareness and knowledge to create *your* own reality and to feel good most of the time, having people around you coming from love and inspiration because that is the vibrational signal that you are broadcasting.

2. The Law of Deliberate Creation

The Law of Deliberate Creation seems clear enough, but is it? To be living the Law of Deliberate Creation, you need to know *what* you want and *why* you want it. But with the thousands of people I've connected with through my work as a coach, mentor and trainer, the majority appear to hold a very clear idea of what they don't want but have no clear awareness of what they *do* want. But regardless of not knowing what you want, the way forward to a life of happy creation is dependent on how you feel at any moment in your life.

Your feelings are all-important

Now, this may seem pretty unimportant, 'airy-fairy' or vague, when you have much bigger fish to fry, such as wanting more money, better health, promotion, a new career or the body you want, but the way you *feel* will always be at the centre of what you create. We usually want something because we know it will help us to feel good when we have it. To deliberately create what you want, you must focus on feeling good first regardless of the conditions around you (more on conditions under Law of Allowing). As you do this, you then become a vibrational match to the emotion you will feel when you get what you want.

By feeling an improved emotion of excited anticipation alongside a positive belief, you emit a vibrational signal that attracts more feelings like it. As you do this and build momentum, the Law of Attraction will bring you more better feeling thoughts, until you feel so good about what it is you want that there is no doubt, no limiting belief, no resistance. Ideas, thoughts and inspiration then flow into your existence matching the vibrational signal that you are now emitting and guide you on your path to take *inspired* action to create what you want. You have, in that moment, become an *Allower* to all that you want.

You have complete freedom to create what you want by giving deliberate attention to where your thoughts, beliefs and emotions, in other words, your vibration is at any moment in time in relation to your desire. Take note and let your emotions guide you in the manifestation process.

3. The Law of Allowing

This all-important law is also known as the Law of Least Resistance. First of all, let's be clear what 'allowing' means. Allowing is when you are feeling good, when you are 'in the flow', when all seems easy and naturally falls into place, when you are in a place of wellbeing. In contrast to allowing, there is resistance, and to name a few of the emotions we feel when we are in this state are fear, doubt, overwhelm, worry, anxiety and despair. If you're not allowing, you're resisting. It really is that simple. At any moment in time, as you are emitting energetic signals, you are either in a place of allowing or resisting, which in easier terms to understand: feeling good or feeling bad. And when you are in a state of allowing (feeling good) you are in vibrational alignment with the energies of wellbeing and inspiration that the Universe is flowing to us at all times. You are then in a state of seeing, hearing, or feeling the impulse to take the inspired actions to manifest what you want to deliberately create.

I want to repeat what I have just written as it is something that is incredibly important to consciously accept: *the energies of wellbeing and inspiration are flowing to you at all times.* It isn't a flow that just stops, it is always flowing to you, like a river flowing downstream. However, there are times when you are in resistance (feeling not good emotions) and you are unable to feel the flow of wellbeing as you are blocking it with the resistant signal you are emitting (remember the Law of Attraction will bring you more of what you are feeling and thinking). However, when you are in a place of allowing and are feeling in alignment with all that feels good, you are a vibrational match to the essence of wellbeing and as such, you receive the wellbeing that is flowing to you. And when you are in that joyous place of feeling excited anticipation from that state of wellbeing, the wonderful desires that up to now you have placed in your imagination will start to (as a consequence of feeling so good) show up in your experience as physical manifestations. It is law.

Reactor or Creator?

We are human and we live on a planet that has much contrast that doesn't please us. We live in a world of so much variety – opinions, experiences, beliefs, thoughts, social conditioning and there will be some aspects you love and want to choose. But there will also be some things you don't like, which is good to acknowledge. However it's not satisfying to stay in that place of displeasure and take it with you for the rest of your life. As you do that, you are in resistance and not in allowing. We're built to feel emotions, and therefore we're developed to feel resistance as we also need to be aware of situations that are not OK for us and to say no when needed. But where we really build resistance is when we stay stuck in a particular situation and build the energy of it even more by giving it more thought and focus.

However, (and this is the great thing) you have a choice as to how you react to what's going on around you. You can stay stuck within a bad experience or you can deliberately choose to prefer another way – a way that feels good. But we are habitual as human beings and a lot of what you do is through habit and you are mostly not even conscious of what you are doing. It is crucial to become aware of how you're thinking and feeling when there is a challenging situation. If you are fire-fighting to put it out, with the more fire-fighting you do, the more focused you are on the fire you are trying to put out, you then bring more of that to you.

So instead, ask yourself how would you like to feel? We can choose to feel better regardless of the condition that we are currently in, and of course, I know there are some situations such as losing a loved one, or experiencing trauma in one's life where this is not easy. However, when we do feel at our unlimited best, we feel the fun, the life, the energy, the vibration, and the connectedness to universal energy flowing through us. Can you choose to start to change the way you think and feel when something that you don't like shows up in your experience? Even a tiny step up the emotional ladder from fear to anger, as an example, is going in the right direction – moving incrementally away from resistance and closer to allowing.

It's also important to recognise what we may be missing out on, by choosing (probably unconsciously) to remain in the clenched fist of an experience, a condition that we have allowed to control our beliefs and behaviours in a resistant way.

When I was about six years old, I asked to take my neighbour's Dalmatian for a walk. Now looking back, that dog was far stronger than me, almost as big as me and instead of me taking it for a walk, it literally dragged me across the pavement the length of the road in which I lived and not only did I end up with cuts, scrapes and bruises, but I carried that experience with me for the majority of my life. I developed a real resistance to dogs. What had essentially happened was that I was initially having a great time taking the dog for a walk and was then 'ambushed' and kept that trauma and used it as a measuring stick for all my interactions with dogs. Excitement had led to trauma...

As a small child, we feel the flow of the joy the excitement, the passion (all coming from that place of allowing) and then, out of the blue, we can have an experience that throws us off and becomes our new emotional set point. We then create resistance around that particular situation. We tune out from any good emotions that we could choose to feel and instead we develop beliefs, thoughts, patterns and habits that don't serve us.

But even with that, the energy flow of wellbeing that is all around us (as consciousness) is still trying to flow through us and when we feel bad, it is because we have disconnected from the flow by feeling the negative emotions. But we're also cutting off from the good feeling emotions, such as joy, love, fun and abundance. We carry the fear of what happened the last time we went from joy to trauma. And if we continue to feel the fear and the anxiety, we tune out and resist. So we need to return to the flow (connecting to that part of us that is all-knowing and all-powerful) and release the habit of thought and behaviour that is continuing to keep us stuck in that old story, by thinking different thoughts that are more empowering and feel better, even if they are tiny steps. We then allow a different response to that experience. And in my case, I have released the fear I had around dogs and now love to be in their company.

This book is to support you in having the tools to release the resistant thoughts and behaviours you have accumulated over your lifetime. You are here to desire, to grow, to evolve and when you're not in resistance, you're in the state of allowing and then ideas can flow to you in a way that feels clear and feels exciting and joyful, but only if you don't do that thing that you keep doing, which is letting past experiences dictate your now experience. You then ramp up the energy of it by telling everyone your old story (sometimes to justify what you're doing now) and keep it focused in the present.

When you do that, you stop your movement forward, you resist and then you're not in a place of allowing in all that you want.

And to add to the swirl of emotions, we judge ourselves for moving out of allowing into resistance and then, as the Law of Attraction kicks in (as it always does – consistent and fair) and gives us more of the resistant thought and feelings we're thinking and feeling, we dig deeper into resistance around that situation!

To be really clear and to make it very simple: when you feel good, you're allowing; when you feel bad, you're in resistance and when you are in resistance, you are blocking the wellbeing, abundance, prosperity and everything that you want from flowing to you. So think about your daily life, the comings and goings that occur throughout a day – some good experiences, some not so good and how do you feel as these occurrences happen? If the experiences are positive, I'm going to take a guess and say you probably feel pretty good, and if the experiences are not so good, I'm also going to guess that you may feel pretty bad. But this is called conditional living – you are not *choosing* your response. In other words, you're swaying emotionally and vibrationally depending on what's going on around you. Sometimes in a state of allowing and sometimes not.

It is your perspective around any situation that is going to decide your experience. If you have an unwanted situation or condition, such as not enough money, by focusing on the stress and anxiety of the bills coming in, you are in a place of resistance by focusing on the lack. If you could instead use that condition as a jumping off place for clarity over what you *do* want instead and focus on the abundance that you do have around you, such as the flowers that are in bloom, the river that is flowing, the sun rising, the sun setting, you can choose to change your lack perspective into one of abundance, thereby altering your feelings and your vibrational output. You are then more consistently in a place of allowing what you *do* want to flow to you, in this case more money. And now, you are living unconditionally, free from conditions and your financial situation dictating your mood and vibrational signal. You are now a creator of your reality, not a reactor to your perceived reality.

4. The Law of Sufficiency and Abundance

When you understand and live from this very important law, all the others fall into place and connect together.

We are unlimited as non-physical beings, and that part of you is always in alignment and always in the state of abundance, as has already been explained in our introduction. It's all it knows. It lives in abundance within you and waits for you, as the physical human being, to move from a feeling of lack and align with that non-physical part of you that is always abundant and which is always aware of the pure potentiality we all hold and can choose to operate from.

But we are also human beings with our own unique personalities, facets, thoughts and dreams. And unfortunately as we were growing up, we listened to those around us, whether they were parents, peers or people who thought they knew better and we absorbed *their* thoughts and beliefs, which for some or most of the time were around the idea of lack or limitation. Remember the 'don't do that' or 'you can't do that' when you were younger – very limiting; and 'money doesn't grow on trees' or 'where do you think we'll get the money to do that?' lack vibration. And as we grow, develop and enter adulthood, we replay and experience these thoughts and beliefs and are then standing like beacons emitting the same signal of limitation and lack, and as explained, the Law of Attraction will bring more thoughts like it and we keep getting the same results.

You create from your beliefs (the vibrational thought that you keep thinking), so if your 'reality' is lack, you receive the same lack, even though the truth of who you are, the unlimited being that is truly you, is flowing through you and only feeling abundance. When the ego, personality part of you feels lack or limitation and the unlimited, non-physical part of you feels abundance and potential, you feel separated and disconnected from the truth of your unlimitedness and you feel tired, resentful, a sensation of one step forward, two steps back. It's when you stop and change the thought pattern of lack that you come back into who you truly are and can connect and tap into the feeling of abundance, and by doing so, attract more abundance to you.

If you're coming from a place that it's never enough, whatever you achieve will never be enough, so when will it be enough? And how will you know when it's enough if you're coming from a place of lack, which is where you are if you are feeling or thinking 'it's not enough'?

However, as I've mentioned, our natural state is abundance and we are all deserving of unlimited abundance, but it's also our perception of how much we deserve which trips us up. It's our personality that puts limits on how much we are worth, depending on the experiences, thoughts and beliefs that we have programmed and which then runs our perception of deserving. We then limit what we believe we deserve, but all the time wanting more. And when we don't receive what we want due to the vibrational signal of our beliefs, we go back into that state of lack and thoughts of 'it's not enough'. What is the current ceiling you have imposed on what you can achieve? What is your current programming telling you?

If you're always looking outside of yourself for the circumstances to be more than they are (more money, more friends, more ease, more time, to name a few conditions we appear to stay focused on) you're not in the present moment appreciating the abundance of what you do have. You then feel more lack and you continue to chase things outside of yourself in order to feel that you *are* enough ('if only I could do this', 'if only I could do that', 'if only he...', or 'if only she...'). When you come from a place right now that you are sufficient, feeling satisfaction and appreciative of where you are right now, then you can peacefully feel that it is enough. It is sufficient. It's the Law of Sufficiency and Abundance.

What story are you telling?

Think of how many times you may have heard or said 'there are not enough hours in the day'. It's likely your focus is then one of lack of time and you are then running a belief programme that time is running out, 'I'll never have enough time to...' and as the Law of Attraction kicks in and responds to this powerful limiting thought and belief, a feeling of overwhelm and stress takes over, the creative part of the brain shuts down and it has then become a self-fulfilling prophecy. As a result, it is then unlikely that you have the creative resources to fulfil the tasks that you had intended. Time is limitless and it's only a practised perception to think the opposite. There are always enough hours in the day – it's what we choose to do with those hours and how we choose to think about those hours that will decide if we feel there is a lack of time or a sufficient amount of time.

'I don't have enough of' is not true. It's a story we tell ourselves and other people. When we can become aware of our limited thinking, we can then choose to direct our thoughts to something that feels better and allow through more of a flow of good feeling thoughts. When you're thinking better feeling thoughts and are aware of a sense of appreciation, it then becomes easier to focus more on the feeling of satisfaction than lack. You cannot attract abundance from a place of lack and limitation.

A limiting behaviour that is becoming prevalent in our society is comparison and this is made easier by the omnipresent social media. There is comparison all around us, from the clothes we wear, the size we are, to the careers that we have and the way we juggle our lives. And the comparison tends to result in a feeling of not being enough! I go into this in greater detail in the chapter Bridging The Gap. How can you allow in the abundance that is your universal birthright if you feel you are dissatisfied with who you are and where you are in your life?

It's very simple to know where you are standing vibrationally at any moment of the day – your emotions guide you. Lack feels bad and abundance feels good. So it is essential that you remain aware of your emotions and what you feel. You *are* sufficient, you *are* unlimited and it is vital that this is remembered. We are hoping that the tools in this book and the downloadable playsheets will help you to not only become aware, but also actively head towards abundance and away from lack of any kind.

5. The Law of Pure Potentiality

The source of all creation is consciousness – the quantum field, the field of pure potentiality. This law may be hard to grasp at first, especially as we use our limited senses to discern and decipher what we want or what we believe we are *able* to attain, but in basic terms, the Law of Pure Potentiality is saying, 'you can have whatever you want', that 'anything is possible'. But to feel the expansiveness of the universal energy, we need to connect to unlimited frequencies and vibrations that feel good. When you are coming from fear-filled or doubting thoughts, you are not connected. In fact, you are limited. But when you feel like you are thriving, or meditating into a peaceful state of connection, you do believe (even if only for a millisecond) that anything is possible. You are then emitting a vibration or frequency of abundance, and allowing the Law of Attraction to bring to you all of what you have created with your vision from this field of pure potentiality.

The pure potential of the Universe can bring you the possibilities, the impulses to take action to achieve whatever you want, but as human beings, the mind cannot conceive of this whole field of unlimited potential. We believe that only what we see is real, only what our senses can perceive is of significance. When we have that experience of swimming or floating in an expanse of ocean with nobody else in sight, we can then sense a feeling of unlimitedness and a connection to all-that-is around us. That is the field of pure potentiality.

And not only is anything possible for *you*, but when you are connected and you believe that *anything* is possible, your own energy will be a positive vibration that can have a ripple effect on the world around you. A quality of life that promotes happiness to those who come into contact with you, and the influence that your clear and expectant vibration will exert over all that you give your attention, to will be exponential.

6. The Law of Detachment

The Law of Detachment, if applied fully in your life, is what will give you the true sense of freedom. This law encourages you to be free of the outcomes of what you are aiming to achieve. It also allows you to let go of the opinions of others, to be free of the stress of what others may feel and thereby freeing you to focus on what feels good for you. By detaching from others' perspectives, you are able to have more clarity over what *you* want and allowing what *you* desire to flow to you by not being in a state of resistance and being side-tracked by other people's feelings, emotions, beliefs and expectations.

When you practise the feeling of disconnection from the expectations and views of people around you and start applying detachment, your life starts to take on elements of peace, joy, delight and you are then connected with your higher self and the energies of the Universe. Decide what you want to create from that open expansive place. But the key is to then detach (let go) from the outcome and enjoy the ride! Remember, our minds are limited and we are not, so by detaching from the limited outcome that our mind can conceive, you open yourself up to the unlimited possibilities that are in the field of pure potentiality, and by trusting in the process, what you desire can flow to you in so many joyful and fun ways that weren't even on your limited radar!

The Law of Detachment says '*in order to acquire anything in this physical universe, we must relinquish our attachments to it*'. As human beings, through concern that we may not achieve a certain outcome, we have a desire to control and we feel that it's our job to figure out how, why, when, who, and in this attachment we become fearful, anxious and we are then in a place of resistance and not allowing. As coaches, we work with our clients to feel into the possibilities that they can open up to from a place of curiosity and clarity, not fear, panic and attachment. The Law of Pure Potentiality will devise opportunities, and if you allow it, it's the job of the Universe to provide you with the direction and the impulses to show you the path towards it as a cooperative relationship and journey.

The impulse may be a phone call that comes through or bumping into someone you haven't seen for so long but is looking for someone just like you for the exciting project they have started. Or you get the impulse to go to a place that starts you on a new exciting journey that you have wanted for a good while. You receive the indicators to show you the best route to what you want. When you are clear about the outcome you want and detach from the anxiety of the 'how' and 'what if', you allow it in the most perfect timing. When you push against by trying to control the outcome, it takes so much longer and becomes the harder route. But when you go with clear intent and the flow of your desire, experiencing curious detachment from the specific outcome that you want and pay attention to the universal urges around you, it happens naturally and with much more ease.

Detachment and my eye!

A clear example of this happened for me about two years ago, and by asking for a solution and detaching from the outcome instead of trying to know or decide the solution coming from anxiety, saved the vision in my right eye. It was a weekend and I was working at a training event this particular Saturday and Sunday. I had gone out after work on the Saturday evening for a couple of hours to meet up with a few mums that I hadn't seen for years from my daughter's old secondary school. As I was looking at the menu, I couldn't focus at all on the print – it seemed blurred and very strange. I couldn't put my finger on it. Walking home that evening, it seemed as if there was a curtain coming down over half of the vision in my right eye. It was pretty scary and pretty weird all at the same time. I didn't have a clue what was wrong, but I just *knew* something was definitely wrong. I hoped that after sleeping that night the vision would clear, but it wasn't to be.

My husband who was working night shifts that week said he would take me to hospital in two days' time, on the following Monday, but I really *felt* (had a strong impulse) that after going into work on the Sunday, I should immediately go into an Accident & Emergency department of a specialist eye hospital in London. But I also allowed myself to be swayed by others' opinions of 'don't bother the doctors', 'wait until Monday' and 'go to the opticians'. This was all replaying in my mind on Saturday night in bed, making it very difficult to decide on my course of action, and on the Sunday morning I asked the universe for help with my decision and then I let go of the outcome, trusting that I would be directed by an energy far more powerful than the limitation of my thoughts and others' beliefs.

As I was travelling into work on the Underground system the next morning, I was sitting randomly looking at the advertisements on the trains (something I never do, as I normally read) and I looked up and right in front of me was this huge brightly coloured advert for a summer holiday with a drawing of a signpost pointing in a direction with the word **HOSPITAL** written on it that you just couldn't miss! I knew in that moment that after work that day I was going straight to the A&E department of the eye hospital. The sign was too obvious to ignore.

I had allowed the solution to be shown to me by letting go of the fear I was feeling and the opinions of others. When I arrived at the hospital later that day, instead of large numbers of people waiting to be seen, there was nobody – only myself and doctors. I was attended to straight away and was diagnosed with a detached retina and was booked in for an emergency operation the next morning, because there was nobody on the operating waiting list – something that the emergency doctor couldn't believe when looking at the next day's operating schedule!

When you stop trying to control an outcome, when you stop listening to others' opinions, when you ask for help from the Universe and then detach from the outcome (pardon the eye pun!), you are then allowing countless solutions to make their way to you. You are then free from worry, fear and anxiety, and instead you open your mind and allow the pure potential of solutions to flow to you, guiding you to take action and live a life of ease, peace, joy and far greater success than your mind can conceive.

7. The Law of Polarity

This law is *the* law to understand for us as human beings living in the physical world and wanting to create a life that feels good. This law explains that duality exists and there are two ends of the pole to every subject and in between there is a spectrum. Polarity represents the two extremes of the same thing. So, some examples would be: hot and cold, right and wrong, strong and weak, abundance and lack, self-pity and empowerment.

Now, this may seem obvious but we are mostly unaware of it when we go about our daily lives, hoping that we are going to achieve what we want. Again, using the Law of Polarity, we tend to focus on what we *don't* want (the opposite end of the stick to what we *do* want). This awareness is incredibly important in creating and manifesting that which we desire. If you want more money but you're focusing on the *lack* (not enough) of money, how can you then be manifesting the polar opposite, which is abundance of money? Remember the Law of Attraction is bringing you more of your vibrational frequency, or vibrational set point, so if you are focusing more on the lack of money and shoring up that frequency by telling friends that you need more money, or worrying about not enough money, the Law of Attraction is going to bring more of that into your awareness. You can't be focused on one end of the stick (lack or need) and attract the opposite end of the stick (abundance).

What end of the stick are you on?

If you ran through your day, how many times do you think more about the opposite of what you *do* want, and then you're disappointed that it hasn't worked out the way you wanted it? For example, you have a busy morning knowing that you have to get the children ready for school (on time) and get yourself ready and into work (on time). The usual routine is stressful and rushed and although you might wake up and *hope* that things may be different this morning, your *dominant* thought is more of how things usually are (and ironically that's why we want the change in the first place!) and then the opposite of what you would love to happen occurs. And yes, you've guessed it – the pattern continues as it always has, *until you start to change the direction of your focus towards what you do want and away from what you don't want.*

It's important to acknowledge what end of the stick you are usually on regarding every subject. When you have awareness, you can start to make change and then feel good as the direction of your thoughts head more towards what you do desire. Not because you have it at this present moment, but *just because* it feels good to imagine, visualise and start to believe the presence of this thing you want showing up in your life.

It is so exciting to understand that you have the ability to choose your perception on any subject, from lack to abundance, from sadness to joy. It is all about the intention you have and the emotion behind that intention. If you are focusing on more abundance and can feel the fun of the abundance and detach from the outcome, you are in a place of allowing what you want to flow to you. However, if you want abundance from a feeling of desperation, you will be attracting more of the lack that you are trying to move away from. Coming from a state of '*why* I want something' and connecting to that purpose and drive, instead of 'how am I going to get it?' which introduces resistance and fear, will literally pay dividends in you moving up the vibrational scale and connecting to all that feels good and allowing your desire to flow.

All of these laws are interconnected and by understanding how they work individually and collectively and practising them in your daily life will not only bring about great movement forward in the way you want your life to be, but will also bring about personal growth that will be exponential. This growth is what you're on this planet to experience – that is the juice of life and is the fun that is yours to be had!

MYTH DEBUNK: You create what you want *only* by understanding the Law of Attraction.

MANIFESTATION METHOD: Become familiar with the universal laws written here. You create what you want through your attention to the Law of Attraction *in connection* to the other universal laws.

Enjoy practising your connection and understanding of these laws by downloading the playsheets here:
www.playsheets.16seconds.co.uk

In the next chapter, Pam will be showing you who we are physically and how we think and behave has a direct impact on what we manifest within our lives. In addition, how creating what we want comes from an awareness of *both* vibrational law and physical responses.

CHAPTER 2
Who You Are Physically

"All truth goes through three stages.
First it is ridiculed. Then it is violently opposed.
Finally it is accepted as self-evident."

– Schopenhauer

Pam

I want to bring you some different types of information in this chapter that are helpful in terms of knowing more about what you might not know so you can work smarter with the Law of Attraction.

I'm fascinated by our bodies, our minds, what makes them work, how one impacts on the other and how all of that can affect the results we get in our lives.

We all operate differently and some people might like the biological information whereas others may prefer the energy information, and some will, like me, be interested in both. So as you read through remember that it only takes one new thing that resonates with you that you start focusing on, initially for 16 seconds, in order to start making a difference with your energy and the Law of Attraction.

I want to introduce you to the five layers of the energetic body; they are physical, etheric, emotional, mental and spiritual energy.

The Physical Energy Body - is the layer that we see in the mirror and recognise as us. Although it is made up of flesh and bone it also has an energetic vibration the same as the other layers which are unseen.

The Etheric Energy Body - The second layer of our energy body is approximately 0.25-0.5 inch from the physical body. And those who see energy and auras have said it feels 'webby' and is sticky and stretchy looking. The etheric energy body has also been referred to as the blueprint of the physical body.

The Emotional Energy Body - The third layer is our emotional energy body and is where we keep our feelings. It is here where both our fears and joys reside and it can be quite volatile at times when experiencing emotions. This is the area we want to free up and flow from.

The Mental Energy Body - is the layer where our creativity and ideas are stored along with our belief systems, personal truths and perceptions, based on our experiences, as well as where we assimilate our thoughts.

The Spiritual Energy Body - is the final layer. It has been said to be the place where our 'consciousness' or 'higher awareness' resides.

You may find it useful to think about your different energy bodies and what might be holding you back in each of them. Historically, emotionally, my challenges have been anxiety, fear and some depression; physically – arthritis; and mentally – limiting beliefs and self-doubt.

Cells and vibrations

> *"Wisdom is knowing what to do next;*
> *virtue is doing it."*
>
> – David Starr Jordan

Quantum science tells us (as does Neuro Linguistic Programming) that our outward experience in life is a reflection of our inner reality, beliefs, thoughts and experiences and how we handle them. Energy medicine experts say that if we aren't experiencing flow in our bodies we can't experience flow in our lives.

David Hawkins MD, PhD backs up what Sandra said in chapter 1 that every emotion has a vibration as does every thought, act, belief and thing in the Universe; anxiety, fear and depression are a low level vibration, which if we are looking at the Law of Attraction, means you can only have that which matches your vibration.

In public, in my 20s and early 30s, I hid my demons well. I pasted on a smile, but life inside my head and at home was hard work. I was exhausted, worked too many hours, didn't earn much money, lived from week to week, felt emotional most of the time, had huge blind spots and just couldn't see an end to it.

Being introduced to a wonderful psychologist in my 30s through a friend of mine was the start of this amazing journey of growth and learning to change my negative patterns. He helped by showing me how to challenge my negative thinking through simple exercises, such as noticing what I said to myself as often as I could, stop, pause and then reframe the negative chatter.

So for example, if I was saying I was stupid because I had taken a wrong turn when driving, I was to notice it, breathe, be forgiving, kind and say something like, "Ah, this isn't the way I wanted to go, so I'll just go a bit further up the road and then do a U turn. I'll remember not to take this turn next time."

I know it might sound silly or obvious, but if you were in the car with a friend or loved one and they took a wrong turn, would you shout at them and call them stupid? Or would you say something reassuring?

Anyway, it worked really well for me. That was years ago, so I was delighted to notice, only this week, when I caught myself doing something 'incorrectly', that I stopped, smiled and was kind to myself. This was and still is a huge step forward for me compared with how unkind I used to be to myself, and proves that practice creates a new neural pathway. Which in turn forms a new habit and it starts with a conscious 16 seconds focus.

"If you only keep adding little by little it will soon become a big heap."

– Hesiod

I was a willing student, I did all the activities that he gave me and I started to see change happen. It wasn't fast, but as I managed to feel less hopeless and depressed, so new opportunities started to come my way as if by magic and each of the work opportunities paid more money than ever before. I had been wishing for more, but with my vibration at such a low level I wasn't energetically ready or willing to allow what I wanted into my life.

And here's the surprising thing: if what I said I wanted had presented itself earlier on, there's no way I would have recognised or been able to hold on to it. Which fits with this saying:

'You can't be more or have more than your self-image of yourself.'

We all have a self-image ceiling and when it comes to allowing 'more' into our lives, be it money, love, health or anything else we desire, we won't allow in or accept that which doesn't match our subconscious self-image of ourselves, as Sandra explained in the Law of Allowing in chapter 1.

And that self-image ceiling vibrates as an emotional state and if you try to get or hold on to anything above that vibration, because you don't (subconsciously) believe you deserve or are worthy of it, you'll probably self-sabotage and stop yourself from keeping it.

Subconsciously I was a bit depressed, anxious, had poor health some of the time but never took a day off work, a people pleaser, rescuer, dependable, tired, exhausted, hopeless and angry a lot of the time.

To the outside world, I looked 'happy', confident, busy and successful. I need to point out that in spite of this, I had a wonderful husband, family and friends, a roof over my head and enough to eat, so the above isn't a complaint, it's just how I felt at the time, which meant I wasn't in a state of allowing.

In her book *The Molecules of Emotion*, Candace Pert not only explains the biology of how cells work and are produced but also how our thoughts and beliefs affect our cells, the reproduction of them and the physical and literal results we get in our life. The following is my interpretation of what I have read, you can always purchase the book or audio to get a better understanding of the science behind her work if it appeals to you.

She explains that 300 million cell divisions occur every minute and that 2% of our blood cells die every day and are replaced and every two months we have a new blood supply. We have trillions of cells and each one has around 70 different receptors on its face and the life of a cell is determined by which receptors are on its surface and whether or not they are occupied by ligands, which are small molecules which bind to the receptors. This binding changes its shape and activity allowing it to transmit a signal to produce change inside the cell.

The hypothalamus produces peptides which are determined by what you think and feel, and as you started to read about in the last chapter, *every emotion you experience is duplicated.* The peptides are channelled to the pituitary gland and then into the bloodstream where they visit all 20-30 trillion cells in your body (10,000 cells can fit on the head of a pin). They then dock on to the cells and create minute physiological phenomena that can translate into large changes in behaviour, physical activity and even your mood. When they dock they take control of all the cell's activities including whether they will divide or not and the composition of the new cells.

Dr Pert was involved in *What the Bleep*, a controversial short film (2004), and said new cells are not necessarily a clone of the old ones being replaced, they reproduce themselves based on the emotions the previous one experienced. If that was depression, then you'll produce more depressed cells. In one hour you produce approximately 18 billion new cells, so if you've been feeling depressed for that hour you'll have more cells calling out for more of that emotion. The same goes for all your other emotions.

What interests me is that every day millions of our cells die and new cells are reproduced. According to Dr Pert's[1] work, the new cells don't have to be the same as the cell that just died. Assuming this is true, doesn't that suggest that if we have ailments or illnesses we should be able to 'cure' them or 'get rid of them' if we produce new cells that are free of the old physical problem? And yet we don't seem to, we appear to 'get worse' the longer we have a condition. As Sandra mentioned previously, we get lazy, put up with how things are, stay in our comfort zone rather than step up and look for what we want.

In my immediate family, arthritis is the key disease; in some of my extended family it's cancer. And since I was a child I've known that arthritis is the big bad disease on my dad's side (he had it severely, as does my sister and so do I, my brothers to a lesser degree). It forms part of my life story, I used to tell it endlessly, it's in the family, it's in the genes, the story has been told with an air of 'what can you do? It's part of our make-up'. But through some simple practices, I've seen my arthritis reduce.

---

1   Candace Beebe Pert, American neuroscientist and pharmacologist who discovered the opiate receptor, *Molecules of Emotion*

On my mum's side the men had heart attacks quite young, the women lived to an old age and eventually cancer took them. We all have our family medical history, stories passed down to us from our elders telling us that what runs in the family can't be changed. It's in the genes, we're helpless, it's hopeless, it's just the way things are.

Yet Pert's work seems to suggest our medical history doesn't have to be fixed; she seems to suggest we can alter our cells depending on what emotions we are feeding our cells and feeling most of the time. This sounds like the Law of Attraction to me!

"I've come to believe that virtually all illness, if not psychosomatic in foundation, has a definite psychosomatic component. The 'molecules of emotion' run every system in our body, creating a body/mind intelligence that is wise enough to seek wellness without a great deal of high-tech medical intervention."
Candace Pert

Our cells crave, cry out for more of whatever emotion they have experienced most of the time, *"and if we give them positive emotions we can change the formation of the cells and over time change what they produce in our body"*. How exciting is that? And what might you attract into your life if your cells and energy fields were to vibrate at a higher frequency? If you want to change your emotional state from negative to positive, start by becoming aware of how you're feeling; if it's not good, take a deep breath, ask yourself what you want to feel instead then start feeling it. We can change our emotional state in seconds if we choose to. Then practise it for 16 seconds, then keep practising it.

Energy psychology

"To love oneself is the beginning of a lifelong romance."

– Oscar Wilde

Dawson Church, a scientist, wrote *The Genie in Your Genes* which is worth reading. He explains why your genes do not have to determine your physical health. That the genetic 'deck of cards' you were dealt at birth does not mean you have to inherit them. Church's work offers us a new way of thinking and a paradigm shift from the old way of thinking that we have no choice. This new science is called Epigenetics.

I've noticed in my one to one coaching sessions that stress has become a big factor. Where once a client's goals were more tangible, often now they involve managing emotional states such as stress. Chronic stress can reduce lifespan, cause illness and promote shortening of telomeres, which are protective caps at the end of DNA molecules that make up our chromosomes, bringing on the signs of ageing faster. A study of mothers taking care of chronically ill children compared to those looking after healthy children found that their telomere shortening suggested they had aged at least 10 years more.

This information helped me change my vibrational state, by reminding me that when I get emotional about something I have no control over, if I stay there too long my cells will want more negative emotions, my telomeres will shorten, I'll age faster, my immune system will also be affected and my body will produce cortisol instead of DHEA (the natural youth drug). Remembering this helps me change my state fast. Thank goodness for vanity I say.

Meditation

Meditation and stress management have been shown to dramatically reduce the impact of stress and improve one's mental health and it doesn't have to be a long meditation. Ten minutes or so is very beneficial; when I am in a hurry I have an 11-minute meditation, but even starting with one or two minutes is valuable and can raise your vibration.

Many years ago, a dear friend introduced me to transcendental meditation. This played a big part in changing my life along with the psychologist's work. The first time I tried it I was nervous, but it relaxed me so much I left the introduction session feeling amazing, rested, at peace and energised all at the same time. You might enjoy it or you may have a different or better meditation technique for yourself. I've tried loads over the years and currently have one I enjoy. If you don't already, it may be beneficial for you to consider finding out more about daily meditation.

One of my clients told me how she tried to meditate but just couldn't. She attended meditation classes but struggled to follow the 'rules'. She really wanted to meditate but wasn't enjoying it. I talked her through one of my favourite quick bio-energetic grounding visualisation exercises which lasts two minutes and she loved it. It's all about finding the right one for you. My belief is that it's important to trust yourself when it comes to what you like and what you don't like.

As Deepak Chopra, author and alternative medicine advocate says, it is important to enjoy the practices we choose to do, be they exercise or meditation. If we don't enjoy them, the good they could do may be outweighed by the lack of enjoyment. And of course the vibration around the practice will be coming from a place of lack rather than abundance.

"Action may not always bring happiness, but there is no happiness without action."

– William James

There's a statement that so many people tell me they dislike: 'fake it 'til you make it'. I understand, it's the fake word, I'm not very keen on it either, but I decided to make it mean 'what do I want to feel mentally and physically that isn't natural for me right now that I need to practise?' And when I was able to answer that question, I'd practise what I wanted that wasn't currently natural until it was. This is how habits are formed, practising something new until it becomes natural, comfortable and part of our unconscious behaviour.

Words have energy associated with them. When I deliver training on goal setting, I ask audiences how many of them like the word goal. Sometimes as many as 50% don't like the word or are neutral. So I ask them, "What would you like to call it instead? Aim, objective, target, dream, desire, ambition? Something else? It doesn't have to fit the dictionary definition, it just needs to be a word that means 'I want to do something about this'." Doing this exercise changes the feeling associated with the word and in turn the vibration.

Here are some other words clients have disliked until they changed them:

> Presentation – sharing information
>
> Commitment – choosing to
>
> Responsibility – deciding I'd like or want to

Maybe you can think of some words associated with your goals that cause you to feel negative physically and mentally. Even if you can't right now, start to notice how your language makes you feel when you think or write about what you want. If you notice a word doesn't make you feel positive, change it or the meaning of it. Doing this simple exercise changes your body language, self-talk and energy around the word or goal. Which in turn creates a vibrational shift.

I hope you are beginning to see there are some simple things you can choose to do, which are in your control, that could help with stress levels and make a difference to your vibration.

Take a moment to think about the implications that your thoughts, beliefs and emotions have on your physical body as well as your mental state.

This new way of thinking presented to us by scientists and energy psychologists aims to break the old paradigm that everything is the fault of the genes and 'out of our control'. My belief is that there is always a way forward, always a way to change things. Your goals are possible if you believe they are, allow time for them to happen and take appropriate action.

> *"Whether you think you can or you think you can't –*
> *you're probably right."*
>
> – Henry Ford

Think of Henry Ford (creator of the Ford car) and Thomas Edison who we associate with the origin of the lightbulb. Each time they failed, they stated they'd found another way not to attempt again. It's that kind of thinking that helped people create airplanes and now we take it for granted we can fly. Instead of letters we can receive emails and texts instantaneously. Wild ideas are how the Internet, computers and mobile phones were created. Big ideas are how the world has changed and developed and how it will continue to change and develop. Candice Pert, Dawson Church, Bruce Lipton and all the other wonderful scientists and researchers out there who have made their way into the personal development world are showing us, through research and science, that there is a new way of thinking emerging. It takes time to permeate and take over the old way, but it's real and it's growing and if more of us practise it we can help to make positive change happen quicker.

If you're carrying old conscious and subconscious hurts and wounds from the past they will show up in your body. Perhaps a knot in your stomach, lump in your throat or pain in your shoulder. Your body tries to communicate with you on a regular basis, sending you messages often ignored or pushed away. Sue Mortimer, author of *The Energy Codes (Your role in creating your life)* says: "The soul speaks to the body, the body speaks to the mind and the mind doesn't listen."

Do you listen to your body? Start noticing what it's trying to communicate on a daily basis. In order to start getting what you want from the Universe you need to align the energy flowing through your mind and body with the energy of the goal you desire.

David Hawkins – Energy levels

"The Universe is change; our lie is what our thoughts make it."

– Marcus Aurelius

David Hawkins tells us if we want to improve our lives and wellbeing from a material as well as mental, emotional and physical place, we need to be aware of the baseline vibrations we're operating from so we can move them upwards.

To get a rough idea of where your baseline vibration is, pay attention when you are under pressure or stress as this will help you work out what your natural response to problems is. Being aware you become fearful or overwhelmed or something else when you are stressed allows you an opportunity to choose to change it. In doing so you start to move your vibration upwards.

Here's my example: in the beginning when I was training to be a coach I'd operate from a vibration of fear before each session, my mind chatter would ask unhelpful questions such as:

- What if I'm not a good enough coach?
- What if I don't ask great questions?
- What if the client thinks the session is useless?

I needed to be operating from a vibration of neutrality, presence and positive energy; remember coaching is all about the client and it's important there's no transference from my world into theirs.

To change the vibration of the situation I decided to become aware of my state (fear), ask myself what I wanted to feel instead, take a deep breath, remember a time when I felt neutral, present and positive (if you don't have an experience of the state, think of someone you know who does and use it), do a mini meditation and then start practising the positive state before each session.

This simple technique is something I continue to practise regularly when I notice I'm feeling a lower energy state. You'll find the downloadable playsheets 1 and 2 helpful in moving you towards a positive state quickly.

Here are some low energy states:

- insecurity, fear, apathy, unworthiness, guilt, depression, despair, powerlessness, grief, anger, revenge, jealousy, hate, rage, worry, blame, discouragement, doubt, disappointment, frustration, irritation, impatience, overwhelm, boredom, pessimism.

You may be able to think of others. All of these levels have their place when life throws us curve balls. Sometimes the pain can drive us on so we can learn, move on, develop and grow.

High energy states:

- courage, hopefulness, contentment, positive expectation, happiness, enthusiasm, eagerness, joy, empowerment, appreciation, freedom, love, passion, gratitude, peace, calm, acceptance.

Dr Hawkins says there's a huge transition when we move from the first list to the second. For me it's true because when I noticed how fearful I was (generally) and recognised I wanted more courage, I set an intention to move towards it with wonderful results.

Something to consider

When we make the decision that we are going to change our vibration and move up the scale, Greg Kuhn, a quantum physicist, says we need to move through the energy states one step at a time.

If your true unconscious operating vibration around a goal or particular area of your life is fear, sadness, numbness, feeling disconnected or some other negative emotion and you want to jump to joy, it can only be momentary – it is unsustainable, the leap is too far in one go and there is a chance you will bounce back to your 'natural' state.

According to Kuhn, *How Quantum Physicists Build New Beliefs*, long-lasting change and energy shifts become possible by moving into the emotion 'one up' from your current operating one. I see this as a nervous individual climbing up a ladder, taking one rung at a time until they feel steady enough to climb to the next rung, and with practice eventually be at the top of the ladder, able to hold on with ease.

So one way to move up the ladder is to set a realistic goal for who you are right now and be honest about how you feel about it. Write the goal down (if it's too easy it's probably not a goal, more a habit or something you're not too bothered about). Make sure it stretches you a bit.

Write down the emotional state you are feeling:

Is how you feel the desired emotional state required to achieve the goal?

If not, what state do you need to be feeling?

If you find you feel bored by your goal, maybe because you've 'failed' at it before, but want to feel hopeful, admit how you feel then set a goal to start feeling hopeful.

So for me, I'd remember a specific time in the past when I felt hopeful (*you can insert your state here*), and as I remembered it I'd notice what it felt like, what images I held around it and what I was saying to myself. Then I'd practise the feeling daily. Before I knew it, I genuinely felt hopeful about my goal.

The above is a good example of 'fake it 'til you make it'. You want to feel hopeful in the future but at the moment you feel bored. By identifying what hopeful means, looks like, feels like, you can choose to step into it and start practising it until it becomes natural.

Bruce Lipton – Your mind is greater than your genes

Bruce Lipton tells us that *"each atom has its own distinct frequency, or vibration. And quantum physicists study the energetic effect when atoms collide, not their 'matter'. What they see is that when two atomic waves meet, they either meet in sync, creating a constructive or harmonious effect, or they meet out of sync, creating a destructive effect in which they annul each other."*

He goes on to give us a simple example to explain the above that you can try for yourself: *"If you drop two equal pebbles at exactly the same time into water, from the same height, they will both produce the same wave ripples, ie their waves will be in harmony with each other, and when their ripples meet, the combined effect will be an amplification of the wavelength – in other words the merged waves become more powerful. But if you drop the pebbles from different heights or a millisecond apart, then when the resultant waves meet they will not be in harmony and will cancel each other out – the waves become weaker."*

This is an easy way to remember we need to align our personal frequency with the frequency of the goal we desire in order to allow it into our life.

Allowing things to come to us

Esther Hicks says things come more easily to us if we'd just chill out. A mistake we make is wanting something but then creating tension by holding on to it too tightly because of a mental anxiety around having to have or get it.

She tells us to connect with the energy frequency of the goal (be it love, passion, fun), and practise stepping into that feeling, starting with 16 seconds (and building up to 68 seconds), each morning when we wake up, before we start thinking about what the day holds.

By getting the momentum going we will create a different type of day. Everything we want is already out there, we just need to tread the path of least resistance by allowing ourselves to feel good about what we want and then allow it into our life without being overly attached as mentioned in chapter 1, Law of Detachment.

In my coaching mentoring advanced training level, my mentor says if you have a decision you're finding hard to make, and find yourself standing still and doing nothing, pick one of the choices you have and try living as if you've decided this is the right choice for you for three days and see what that feels like. Then if you like, pick the other choice, live in that state for three days and then see which you prefer and want to bring into your life.

Emotional states we experience as adults, on a day to day basis, often originate from past experiences that happened when we were children at a time in our lives when we had no control. Such experiences may have set up feelings and thoughts of rejection, abandonment, not good enough, helplessness or hopelessness. These feelings and their vibrations follow us into adult life and very likely impact on the outcomes we get.

A great first step towards changing your vibration is to work on accepting and loving yourself whilst continuing to develop and grow into an even 'better' version of yourself so you can allow what you want into your life. Working with Hawkins' or Kuhn's ideas on how to shift your energy vibration could be a good starting place.

So to change your vibration, you need to:

- Be honest where you're starting from and own the true vibrational state
- Set a realistic goal and know what vibration your goal requires
- Work towards the new vibrational state
- Practise regularly
- Celebrate all forward movements

The new science

Quantum physics tells us we are made of energy not matter, as is the Universe, as are all things we consider solid and 'real'. But this idea isn't as new as you might think – Socrates posited it as did ancient rishis in India before that. However, in the late 17th century Newtonian physics became the accepted norm based on the theory that there is only matter, and that is the belief system many find themselves believing, operating and vibrating from on an everyday basis. You may have heard of people who believe 'only what we can see is what is real', but what if that's not true? Sure, it's easy to believe in something solid you can touch, feel or see, but what about electricity, what about thoughts? You can't see them but they are real. And quantum scientists tell us everything is made up of energy waves, sound and light, and things appear and look different because of the energy levels they're vibrating at.

Quantum physics has helped us accept that when we look into atoms, they are just energy waves with an invisible force field emitting waves of electrical energy, without substance or reality because they're made of electricity; and of course we know that we're made up of atoms, and that every cell in our body has its cells lined up with a positive and negative voltage inside and out. From this comes the idea that the Universe is one big ball of electrical energy, hence the birth of the Law of Attraction idea that whatever you put out into the Universe it will send back to you, both positive and negative. You may know it as Chi, Qi, soul, essence or spirit.

MYTH DEBUNK: All you have to do is think positively, visualise and the Law of Attraction will work. This myth has disappointed too many people for too many years.

MANIFESTATION METHOD:

- Become aware of what you don't want and then change it into what you do want then take regular and consistent **action**!

- Challenge and change negative mind chatter – speak kindly to yourself

- Allow yourself to think and feel lovely, joyful thoughts to create calm and harmony – 'fake it 'til you make it'

- Breathe in the state you desire and out the one you don't

- Meditate – daydreaming is a form of meditation, start with a minute

- Pay attention to your body and the messages it's trying to give you through feelings; acknowledge, change and practise them for 16 seconds

- Conscious positive thinking is not enough, be honest about how you're feeling then change it

- Keep asking yourself: "how can I move myself up the emotional vibrational ladder?"

- Remember it need only take one new technique, practised initially for 16 seconds, in order to start making a difference with your energy vibration and the Law of Attraction. As you go through the book and downloadable playsheets, collect ideas or techniques that appeal to you.

Questions to ask yourself at the end of this chapter:

- Which of your energy bodies requires some attention?

- Which emotions are you feeding your cells on an hourly basis?

- Negative emotional states cause disease and aging. How can you interrupt yours?

- To meditate or not to meditate, what are your thoughts?

- What words do you often use that don't feel positive? I gave you the example of goal

- What's your baseline vibration when you get stressed? Fear, overwhelm, calmness or something else?

I love learning about new and old techniques when it comes to moving my vibration up the ladder towards a happier and more joyful life.

I find it invigorating and exciting that there's so much research 'out there' to be considered, some old and well tested, some newer. What research resonated most with you? Bruce Lipton, Candice Pert, Dawson Church, Dr Hawkins?

I'm so happy I found techniques that work for me, it was so exciting to notice the changes as they started appearing in my life, they motivated me to 'keep up the good work'.

Go to www.playsheets.16seconds.co.uk to download the playsheets for this chapter.

In the next chapter you'll learn more from Sandra about how the larger vibrational part of you creates your reality from the field of all possibilities to support you to live a life of pure potentiality.

CHAPTER 3
Who We Really Are Vibrationally

Sandra

It's very easy to believe that we are only the physical flesh, blood and bones that we can see in the mirror every day. In fact, our world and society continually reinforce this by focusing on how well our bodies are *performing* (or not), achieving what we want through hard thought out *action* (our brain's thought processes that work for us or against us) and consistently reminding us to keep physically *doing* in the stressful workload of life.

No wonder we feel limited and stressed and no wonder we believe that this is all there is. But there is far, far more to this person that is you and far more to your ability to achieve what you want to be, do or have. And on a very deep level, you know this. I am hoping that this book will help you to remember how it felt when you were very young, before you allowed your consciousness to listen to parents, peers and society. A time, long ago, when you were clear about who you truly were (and still are) and you had certainty about your ability to have anything you wanted. So, let's break down the myth that the physical body is everything and let's be clear who and what your physical body really is and the unlimited potential it holds by focusing on the true reality of who you really are – your vibrational self.

Without going into too much detail (or it could become a book in itself!), the *average* human body, at a very basic level, miraculously contains living cells, tissues, organs, numerous systems such as the digestive and circulatory systems to name just a couple; various biochemical constituents; holds eight pints of blood; consists on average of 60% water and contains a brain weighing around 3lbs, and according to latest research, has a memory storage space of a million gigabytes! And in case you are like me and cannot even begin to understand that size of capacity, it would be the same as your brain holding the recordings of 3 million hours of TV shows and you would need to keep the shows running continuously for more than 300 years to use up all of that storage.

There is no doubt about it – the physical human body is a phenomenon and, for the most part, serves us incredibly well. But there is so much more to who we truly are than just the human body and to know and to understand this opens the door to unlimited possibilities. So, let's start to understand the core and the bigger part of who we are and how it governs us more than anything else.

Vibration and choice

You have an inner being, the vibrational part of you. The all of who you truly are that does not hold any limiting or negative thoughts or beliefs. When you are a child (usually up until around the age of five when negative messages begin to impact our consciousness) you vibrate with your inner being – you are seeking that which feels good. You resonate with curiosity, adventure, fun and ease and you act mainly by instinct, not by limitation and acting on negative thoughts, as can become the pattern as we get older and then forget about that huge part of us that can help us to resonate with all that we truly want to be, do or have.

Your inner being is pure potential, pure vibrating energy and knows what you want the second you recognise it, and not only does it know what you want but it becomes what you want, ready for you to catch up and become a vibrational match to it. There is no assertion with the Law of Attraction. It cannot push on you what you desire. It waits for you to sing from the same hymn sheet as your inner being, and when you become a match to what you want, you are in a place of allowing all that you want to flow to you. Our desire is for this book to show you the tools to change your thoughts, your beliefs and your point of attraction so that you can be a vibrational tower emitting signals that attracts to you all of what you *do* want and not that which you *don't* want.

Your physical body is a powerful tool to gain clarity around what you want and what you don't want. It is the most perfect instrument of focus because you are living in a physical world where conditions are happening around you all of the time. Some of these circumstances are good and therefore you feel good as a result and unfortunately some are not and then you don't feel so good. If this is the case, you then resemble a tree blowing in the breeze, at the beck and call of those situations, allowing them to direct you to feel good or not. And then life becomes a reaction to what is going on around you instead of having some form of control over how you feel, regardless of conditions.

You **do** have the ability to feel good, regardless of what is surrounding you, but it is by knowing that there is more than the physical brain to either support or hinder you in these times and by consciously moulding and shaping your vibrational energy through your thoughts and beliefs, **you** have the freedom and power to control what it is you are feeling and therefore attracting. When you *know* this and implement it, you will no longer be a tree blowing in the random direction of the breeze, but instead you will stand solid with your inner being, in your knowing that conditions no longer need to affect you and you can **choose** your response in all areas of your life. You are then consciously choosing your vibrational frequency – your point of attraction that will support your great visionary self, by bringing the tools you need when you need them as cooperative components with the Universe.

As we are all beginning to understand, especially as science and quantum physics has reinforced, we are all vibrational. Everything is energy (including us humans and including the chair that you may be sitting on, the table you eat at, or this book you are holding) and everything vibrates at a certain frequency, including your thoughts, beliefs and emotions. The Law of Vibration is as real as the Law of Gravity, but we have relied on the saying 'seeing is believing' and unless we can see it, we tend to dismiss it and by doing that we close the door on the most powerful part of who we really are.

You accept the Law of Gravity exists because you don't float up into the air when you step outside and so you therefore believe it.

If you can suspend your belief and open up to the possibility that there could be another way to have the life you want, other than wishing, hoping and relying on hard work, you will begin to know that your vibration and the frequency to which you are vibrating has a direct connection to what you're attracting and manifesting. You can then become free to be a clear and focused attractor of what it is you want to have and feel in all areas of your life.

You have heard the saying 'birds of a feather flock together' or 'like attracts like' and this is due to everything having a vibrational point of frequency that is oscillating and drawing the same vibrational point of frequency to that central point; an easier way to put it is a match to that vibration. Which is great if you are vibrating at a frequency of positivity and a happy, higher emotional state, but not so good if you are feeling negative, unhappy and despondent about any aspect of your life, as your vibrational point of frequency is a match to more of the same. And as you get more of the same, whether that is more of the same thoughts, or more physical evidence to back up that disempowering thought, it becomes a belief that is then programmed in our subconscious and played out again and again in our life.

You become a vibrational match to these beliefs as you are now vibrating from that point of attraction, which in turn strengthens the negative experiences you are living. It then develops into a cycle and a very frustrating way to live, because you consciously want to move forward and have what it is you want, but you are allowing your current thoughts, subconscious beliefs and therefore your vibrational point of attraction to **control** you. So you try to change things around by taking physical action, but because you have the same underlying thoughts and beliefs that question the achievement of what you want, your point of frequency (your point of attraction) is setting you up as a match to the same questioning underlying thoughts and beliefs that are preventing you from having what it is you want. And so you attract more of the thoughts that sabotage you and there's that damn repetitive cycle again!

I was working with a wonderful client who had tried for many years to lose weight and to achieve her ideal weight. She had gone down the conventional route of various diet plans that had come on to the market and had at times successfully lost weight, only to put the weight back on again. It was a constant cycle of weight loss and weight gain, the yo-yo syndrome. I was working with her in one of my group coaching programmes and on one of the group coaching calls she asked me the question, "Why when I get up on a Monday morning and feel really positive that today is going to be the day to start the weight loss plan again and to end the day in a really positive way, do I sabotage it by the Monday lunchtime?" I then asked her the question, "When you wake up with the intention of what you want, do you *believe* you can achieve it?" Her answer was "No."

This was a very clear example of her thought programming which had developed over the years of trying and (in her eyes) failing to achieve what she wanted: her belief that she couldn't succeed was far stronger than her intention and desire to lose the weight. Until that belief is replaced with a repetitive thought (and therefore becomes a belief) that supports her positive intention, she will continue to remain in the yo-yo cycle. This will then lead to further feelings of failure, which will then reinforce the belief that she can't succeed in this area of her life and she will continue to vibrate at that same frequency, attracting more of the actions and thoughts that don't support her. She will remain stuck in this area of her life until she *chooses* a different thought paradigm to change this pattern.

An important thing to recognise is that things don't just happen to or for us. As everything is vibrational energy, everything is cause and effect. Think about it in the most general way, how many times have you, or you've heard someone else, say, 'Oh God, it's Monday' early on a Monday morning in a defeated tone? How many times do you hear that this particular Monday just gets worse and worse? Or that old saying that people repeat when something not so good has happened, 'everything happens in threes' and then they believe that they must be so right when the two other situations occur that then compounds that belief that everything happens in threes. But, it's not a coincidence – you have set the vibrational tone for your day and as everything is energy, you are picking up everything that is an energetic vibrational match to what you are saying and thinking in that moment. And so, as the Law of Attraction brings you evidence of what you're thinking about (such as everything happens in threes), you adopt it as a belief. As one thing has happened, the majority of us are subconsciously programmed to wait and expect the other two situations to show up in our experience.

Think about it. Do you really believe that the amount of times you hear this happening, across the planet, they are just coincidences? There has to be more to it than just coincidence when things happen that appear to be evidence confirming what you think and believe. Things don't happen by accident, we attract it by our thoughts, beliefs and our vibrational point of attraction.

Interestingly, how often when one *wonderful* thing has happened is there the expectation that another two wonderful experiences will follow? Rarely. We are quick to reinforce the negative, but incredibly slow to focus on and shore up the positive. How weird is that? We want to live a happy life but our expectations, in general, resonate more easily with the not having and the negative than the having and the positive.

Let's think about this a little bit. Depending on who you have mixed with in your life, you may have friends or people you know (or you may even be one of these people) that when there is the potential of something good happening for them, for example the possibility of a new job, they will say that they don't want to talk about it in case they 'jinx it'. For anyone that doesn't know this term, it means in case they bring bad luck to this particular situation by speaking about it. Now they (or maybe you) would have said that comment quite unconsciously and as we say what we think and we think what we believe, this is an unconscious belief pattern that is running and controlling the reality that this person is going to manifest as a result of this belief, and therefore their point of attraction.

To say 'I might jinx it' is believing and vibrationally saying, 'I am doubting that this wonderful situation will remain wonderful for me' and then the emotion of doubt has been thrown into this potentially exciting, new phase of life and the person saying and believing this is now vibrating at a perfect match to doubt, and the previously exciting new phase is now thrown into jeopardy. And yet we do this so easily. As adults, we find it so much more difficult to throw our hands up in the air and say 'hell, yes, bring it on!' which would open ourselves up to exciting possibilities by being a vibrational match to the feeling of anything is possible.

Focus

As human beings we are lazy. We move more towards habit and comfort instead of towards expansion and stretch, so when we desire something new, we excitedly plan for it (more money, a new relationship, a new job). But within a very short while you go back to your habitual pattern of thought, 'I know I want this, but where is it?' 'I thought I would have it by now' or 'why is it taking so long?'

And these thoughts are keeping you focused on the *absence* of what you want.

As I have already explained, you are constantly vibrating energy and consistently vibrating a signal out into the expanse of the Universe. As you vibrate the signal of what you're thinking and feeling, the Law of Attraction picks it up and sends you more of the same thoughts and emotions and eventually, physical matching evidence will manifest in your life. So if your thoughts and therefore your vibrational set point are predominantly on the *absence* of your desire, the Law of Attraction will bring you more of the same. As a result, your disbelief about getting what you want becomes stronger and over time (sometimes a very short time) your belief makes it a done deal.

As you believe, so you act and if your beliefs are limiting, so are your actions and so is your ability to believe in change and your unlimited potential. But you do this because you are sometimes unwilling (and too lazy) to stay focused on what you **do** want and unwilling to believe that a different reality could come into your experience, while there is still the physical evidence around you of what you don't want. You are not committed to believe that *you can choose your thoughts and beliefs and therefore control your point of attraction.*

How do you think that you are experiencing any situations that are occurring in your life right now? Because you have thought and focused them into being! It's hard sometimes to take that on. We have become a blame culture and anything that happens we don't like, we find it easier to blame an outside source. We blame friends, family, relationships, work, the economy, the government – anything, rather than us! But it is illogical to think that you can focus on what you *don't* want and receive more of what you *do* want. So just imagine, if you are clear that you don't have enough money and you stay focused on this 'reality', how can you expect a completely opposite vibration of abundance to come into your experience? It can't and won't happen. But instead of giving your power away by blaming inflation, or a double dip recession, you could instead focus on and feel the appreciation for what you **do** have. By practising this, your emotions and your point of attraction are getting ready and you are becoming a closer match to the money that you want.

Whatever is going on in your life, it is already manifested, it's already done. Don't put your attention on what's done, put your attention on where you are going. So when you want something, the best thing is to simply focus on it. Don't give your attention to the absence of it and then take the old habitual route of becoming angry, frustrated, defensive and making up reasons as to why you don't yet have your desire. Don't fall into the trap of thinking the way you've always thought.

Allow change to take place. Let go of impatience for what you do want to show up and instead remember, the habit of negative and lack thinking has been developed over many years, sometimes since childhood. It can take some time to alter this habit, so be kind to yourself and enjoy the process of focusing on and imagining all the wonderful elements you want to bring into the life you want to create.

When you really understand and believe this, it's an empowering realisation to know that you can only attract that for which you are a vibrational match. You can then consciously choose to focus on what you **do** want, regardless of what your physical reality is showing you, and start pre-paving by your thoughts, beliefs and actions for the life that you want. You have the control. You have the power. Be committed to dreaming of and feeling into that new life and don't be lazy by going back to observing and believing in what's currently going on around you. As you had a part in creating the past, so you can create the future.

Emotions play a huge part in your point of attraction

Emotions are what we feel. Emotion is energy, a vibration and it's the language that the Universe understands. It invokes either a good feeling thought or a bad feeling thought and we all vibrate at the level of our feelings. It is the power behind our thoughts. It is the powerful engine that drives the strength of our thoughts and beliefs. And emotion plays a huge part in determining where we are in relation to our point of attraction.

Your emotions are your indicator of where you are in relation to what you want. Your inner being is coming from a place of abundance, appreciation and joy and when you feel any of the lower emotion scale feelings such as worry, fear, anxiety, overwhelm and depression, you have separated from your inner being (that true self) and that separation doesn't feel good. You vibrate with your inner self and when you are vibrating away from it by thinking thoughts that are in opposition to the pure positive thoughts that your inner self thinks, you can feel the disparity and the discomfort and that translates into the lower emotions. It is the same with your thoughts and beliefs. Your inner being is pure, positive, limitless energy, and believes fully in the power of love and your unlimited potential. And when you think anything that is disempowering, you have once again separated from who you truly are and you feel the discord that translates into feeling worry, sadness – any emotion that doesn't feel good.

Knowing how you feel about a thought you're having is hugely important in either moving towards what you want or standing still in what you've already got. A belief is a practised thought and when we first become aware of the Law of Attraction and our part in it, we can get nervous and panicky about what we could be attracting by what we say in the moment. We sometimes want to gobble back something negative for fear that the Universe will hear it and bring to us an exact match of what we've just said. However, *the Universe doesn't hear what you say, it hears what you feel.*

So where do you stand emotionally in relation to what you think and believe about what you want? When you are thinking of more money, are you feeling desperate, worried and anxious (the lack of the money) or are you in sync with your inner self and feel appreciative of all that you do have around you – friends, family, your health (abundance)? Your ability to manifest what you want will be in direct proportion to which end of the situation you are focusing on – lack or abundance. So let's think about emotion in relation to the thoughts and beliefs you have that may be empowering you or limiting you.

If we focus on some empowering thoughts or beliefs, such as 'I'm doing well', 'I love my life', or 'things are always working out for me', what emotion do we tend to feel behind these thoughts? Is it a fist pump in the air, excited about the prospect of moving forward and joyfully excited about tomorrow? Very likely the answer is no. We tend to play down any improvement in how we feel and what we're achieving, either due to the 'embarrassment' of what it may look like if you jump for joy, or as I said earlier we may have a fear that we could 'jinx' it if we speak about it. Or we may be aware of other people around us and how they may be feeling if their life isn't going in the direction they want and so we play down feeling good. Or it may just be that we have grown and developed from very young children to give less attention to what feels good and give more attention to what feels bad! And for these reasons, the emotion behind these potentially good feeling thoughts is likely to be pretty neutral. Think about it, if someone admires what you're wearing, there can be a tendency to say, 'this old thing, I've had it for years!' We play down good feelings and emotions.

So, now let's focus on some disempowering thoughts and beliefs, such as 'I'm stupid', 'No one ever listens to me', 'Life is hard', 'I can't do this', 'I might as well not bother, what's the point?' What do you think the emotion is behind these thoughts and beliefs? You can almost tangibly see the body language and you can almost hear the energy behind these beliefs. There is likely to be very strong negative energy – maybe anger, frustration and disappointment, and in some cases, fear that these feelings will never improve.

It is sad, but it is a fact that when we are expressing a negative thought we animatedly put strong emotional energy behind it, and when expressing something positive we are generally emotionally flat after the initial 10 seconds of appreciation. Think of it like carriages on a train: when you are focusing with positive emotion on what you do want, you are adding carriages in the direction of where you want to go. But when you are feeling strongly negative about a situation that you don't want, you put carriages going in the other direction and then there's a tug of war and you remain stagnant in the middle. Not moving, just standing still.

So knowing that your emotional point of attraction is building momentum on a thought, and knowing the Universe responds to that feeling and through the Law of Attraction will bring you more emotion and thoughts like it, wouldn't it be a good idea to start fist pumping when things are going great and reduce the emotion behind anything that's not going so well? Let's start becoming aware of the emotion that we are expressing when feeling or verbalising a thought. Let's really turn the volume up on excitement, joy, positivity and movement forward and mute the emotional energy behind anything that isn't going the way you want it to right now.

Law of Attraction and momentum

We have already delved deeper into the laws of the Universe, however it's important to recognise here the power that momentum and the Law of Attraction hold in keeping you 'stuck' in your beliefs. As I keep deliberately repeating, a belief is only a thought you continue to think but the Law of Attraction helps you to keep thinking those thoughts. This is really important to know as it will also help you to understand that you're not just being a lazy focuser – well you are, but there are also other factors involved that can make it more difficult to think thoughts that feel better and that can head you in the direction you want to go.

When you think a thought that you don't like or want, such as 'I don't have enough money', you send a thought vibration out into the Universe, and because the Law of Attraction is always working, it will bring back to you more thoughts that are a match to the same frequency that you are emitting. And the feeling of lack will get stronger because you have become a match to more of these same thoughts (remember, you can't focus on lack and receive abundance).

When this happens and it feels like there is no change and the situation is becoming worse, your thoughts and emotions are now at full power focusing negatively on the lack and it becomes bigger and bigger. It builds **momentum**. It is like the snowball effect, like a spinning roundabout that you can't get off, just getting faster and faster. This is what we do on a regular basis: we build momentum on what we don't want. As I mentioned in an earlier chapter, we do it by speaking to our friends about our unwanted manifested reality and we listen while they commiserate and tell us their similar stories. We are keeping what we don't want firmly planted and growing by the attention we are giving to it. We are then a beacon emitting a vibrational signal of all that we don't want and we keep that beacon shining brighter and brighter by the attention we give it, and by building the momentum of our emotions and thoughts around it, the Law of Attraction does its job by bringing more to us of the same.

But as I've said, the Law of Attraction is always fair. Which is great news. It doesn't discriminate where or when it sends a matching frequency. So, if we can build the momentum on what we don't want, we can build the momentum on what we do want and let the Law of Attraction do its job. We usually have stories running through our minds of past failures or what it feels like to not have something we want or something that isn't going well and this sabotages us in achieving what it is we do want, and as you now understand, we are then on a roll and get more of the same.

However, if we can really be open to a new vision – a vision of what we want – and really feel the emotion behind the vision so that we can develop new thoughts and new feelings around our desire, we allow our subconscious mind to develop new pictures and new empowering thoughts about it. As a result, we change our actions into positive, inspirational actions. As we do this, we send out energy, a vibration into the Universe and then whatever is a vibrational match to the inspired, looking forward frequency we are sending out, will reflect back and will show up in our experience. It is Law (of Attraction).

Asking from the best possible state

An important clarification to make here (and apologies for possible repetition, but this is important to clarify) is when you ask for something you want, what state of thought and vibration do you request it from? So, just carrying on with the theme of wanting more money, are you asking from the *need* or the *desire*? It's an important distinction to make because there are two vibrational ends to everything you want. If you are focusing on why you *need* the money, maybe to pay the bills, or to pay for a school trip for your children or whatever, you are asking from a place of lack, a place of need because you haven't got the money. But if you are asking for more to (as an example) appreciate, for more fun, more adventures, your asking is coming from a place of recognising the abundance you already have and you as a beacon will be vibrating from a much clearer, more abundant place because you are not feeling lack. *And remember, wherever you are vibrating is what you are going to get more of.*

Let's just give a couple more examples to be really clear about everything having two opposing ends of the subject. When you are asking a question, you are not in the same vibration as receiving the answer, you are in the vibration of asking a question and therefore will not receive the answer until you stop thinking about the question and instead just focus on the answer. When you are focusing on a problem, you are not in the vibration of finding a solution. How many times will you or someone else you know who cannot locate their keys say 'I've lost my keys' and yet later on in the day will randomly see them and declare that 'I've found them!' As the day went on, you or your friend had been distracted and were no longer in the vibration of feeling they were lost, because if you're focusing on them being lost, you cannot be in the vibration of them being found.

So be aware, when you are wanting to manifest something, are you coming from the vibrational end of the stick that will bring to you what you want or are you coming from the end of the stick that will keep you where you are? The choice is yours and having an awareness of how you think and feel is going to allow you to be aware of what frequency you need to be vibrating at to have it reflected back to you in your reality.

When moving forward into a reality that you want, it is important to not look back at where you were or look at the current situation that you want to change. Your inner self never looks back – it only looks forward. When we are clear about what we no longer want, it is a great jumping off point. It's a catalyst for change. It's a motivator. But the key is to allow it to motivate you for change, *not then stay focused on the circumstance that you want to move away from*. Your job is to be focused on the joy of moving forward, not to separate yourself by thinking thoughts that are in opposition to what you want. Most desires are shot down within a few seconds of it coming into the conscious mind, by thoughts such as 'It's too hard for me', 'It's too big', 'What will people think?' and you retreat back into where you have been, but have yearned to move away from, for a long time.

You start to overthink, you let familiar limiting beliefs take over and because you have already separated yourself from your inner self, you immediately doubt the impulse that had just clearly made itself known about the direction in which you would like to go. You take action from a forced place, a needy place – a place of overcompensating, making it work, forcing it to happen, instead of taking the easier route of lining up with your inner vibrational self and allowing those new pictures of what you want to form in your subconscious, enjoying the fun of feeling into those pictures. Building the wonderful emotional momentum behind it and certainly not taking score of when is it going to turn up. It's going to manifest when you become the attractor of it.

Are you the realiser of what you want?

At this point, I just want to add more clarity in helping you to achieve what it is you want to be, do or have. Think about the following statement as it is really important in the world of manifestation and vibration:

When you want something, your inner self becomes whatever it is you're asking for.

Full stop. The vibrational essence of what you want has manifested because your vibrational self has become what it is you have asked for. **But the question is: are *you* seeing that desire show up in your physical world? Is it coming to fruition?**

And the answer is *no* if you are still beating the drum of old thoughts and beliefs, such as 'I want it, *but…*'. The answer is *yes* if you can suspend limiting beliefs, relax into the fun of the creation process in your regular daydreaming and visualising moments and love the feeling of creation just for the wonderful feeling of being in alignment with your inner self, without the questioning and doubting of where is it now? When is it coming?

Enjoy the process. Have fun. Enjoy the synchronicities of people turning up at the perfect time in the perfect place, the impulse and acting on a thought you get that takes you closer to what it is you want. Allow it all to flow to you, as the Law of Attraction is primed to do once you line up with all of who you truly are. Don't be impatient and instead commit to the journey, the process. If you enjoy building your own home, you are not going to want to miss the fun of the process and just see the finished product. You are always going to want something else, so have fun along the way.

Be patient – it comes incrementally

As I said earlier, when you *really* want something, you tend to look more at the fact that it isn't in your physical reality yet. Even if you are opening up to the possibility that you can create what it is you desire, there is a tendency to be impatient and then switch your focus on to the absence of it showing up. But we now know this leads to a further delay in achieving your desire because you are at odds with your vibrational inner self who has already become what you want and you are therefore no longer a match to what it is you wanted in the first place.

Be aware of this gap in time in the asking for what you want and the receiving of what you want. Remember there are two vibrational ends to a stick, so if you are still asking from a place of lack, you cannot receive. And to receive you need to be in the receiving (the allowing) mode. That mode of feeling good, appreciating, having fun, feeling loving and joyful. It is so important to not take score and start questioning where your stuff is or when is it going to turn up as that takes you away from receiving and into resistance, which will block what you want coming to you. So in the gap of time while you are allowing what you want to flow to you, use the time joyfully, use it wisely. Build your vision, feel the fun of it, feel satisfied as you live your life, feel the excited anticipation of attracting in what you want knowing you are in a powerful state of allowing.

Your thoughts are where you last left them so leave them in a good feeling place. Usually things don't turn around overnight, they happen incrementally as you become more and more ready to be a vibrational match to what you want. As you are in that wonderful state of feeling good and allowing, you will be open to those thoughts that drop into your mind out of the blue (I usually get them when I'm mindlessly cleaning my teeth, when I'm feeling good and not thinking about anything else that could be resistance). These thoughts are *received* thoughts, guidance from your vibrational inner self who has become what you want and, by sending you impulses and thoughts, is showing you the easiest path to follow to get what you want. A *received* thought is different from a thought you *think* – it's an instinctive thought or feeling. It's as if it's randomly appeared while you're walking down the street in a world of your own. This is guidance. Trusting and following this guidance is what will feel good, clear and a knowing that this is the next step to get you to where you want to be.

When you're in a state of resistance (anxiety, fear, worry, doubt) you are not open to this guidance. You have closed down and it doesn't matter how many impulses or thoughts your inner self is flowing to you, you won't hear or feel one of them. And you will stay longer in the absence of what you want. So, it's easy – just feel good!

Just feel good...

Seriously, feeling good and feeling appreciation is when you are lined up with your vibrational self (your inner self) and you are emitting signals that put you in the receiving or allowing mode of what you want to flow to you.

Let's just feel into the word *allowing*: it feels good, it feels easy, it feels open, expansive, joyful, loving and you feel that you are in the flow of the universal energies. Most of us can recognise that we have felt that way at some time in our lives. And because we feel so good, our fair friend, the Law of Attraction, sends us more things or experiences to feel open and easy about and life just gets better and better.

But now let's feel into the word *resistance*: it feels tight, it feels closed, it feels as if a door is closing, barriers are erected, humps in the road. And when you feel resistance, you are closed off from your inner self and the universal energies. You are feeling fear, worry, disappointment, stressed, irritated to name just a few resistant emotions and you are then an attractor of more experiences that will bring you more of those emotions. Resistance happens when the situations you are in are more negatively charged. They feel big. They feel overwhelming. But you're not going to get to what you want from where you are. Taking action through resistance isn't going to get you what you want – allowing is.

A few years ago, I was burned out, feeling resistance and resentment and I decided to take some time away from my business, which I could have felt was pretty scary, as if I wasn't working, I wasn't earning. But I had come to the tipping point where how I felt was more important than what I had. So I decided to spend the next few months (or however long it was going to take to feel better) to look for things to appreciate. Literally. I devoted my time to finding joy, and when I did find it, to appreciate it. As I committed to this and my vibration (my inner self) naturally lined up with this, the Law of Attraction brought me many examples of where I could appreciate with joy.

A few days into this commitment, I went to a coffee shop close to where I lived and was enjoying and appreciating a good cup of coffee while I was writing my appreciation journal. As I was sitting there, out of the corner of my eye there was this beautiful, approximately three-year-old French girl with a bunch of brown curls just sitting there with her legs swinging from where she was sitting on a chair that was too big for her. Her father had bought her a cookie and he asked her why she wasn't eating her cookie and she replied that she was waiting for her hot chocolate. She wasn't impatient for her drink, she was just quietly looking around, her big eyes wide with anticipation and excitement and then her hot chocolate arrived. To watch the joy she felt as she took a small bite of her cookie and a sip of her drink brought tears to my eyes. I can still remember the feeling of joy I felt watching her – pure, unlimited, joyful energy in motion. It was an absolute gift and matched exactly the feeling of joy that I had declared I wanted to feel, and I allowed myself to be guided to that café at the perfect time with the perfect example of joy sitting there waiting for me because I had no resistance to finding what I wanted.

Everything that comes back to you is a result of your vibrational output. So have clarity around what you want to achieve, how you feel when you think about it and have fun along the way. Stay away from negativity, keep positive friends close and appreciate, appreciate. We always have one thing we can appreciate, so find it, focus on that sense of appreciation and have fun in the process of creation. This is *your* life and it's time to live it!

MYTH DEBUNK: You manifest what you want *only* by being aware of your thoughts.

MANIFESTATION METHOD: Create what you want by paying attention to the larger part of you – the vibrational, energy part of you. How does that part of you feel? Focus your thoughts and attention on what you desire only when you are in a state of vibrational ease, clarity and peace (a good feeling place), not when you are in a stressed vibration of lack (a state of resistance).

Enjoy recognising the huge importance of who you are vibrationally and how to play with your vibration in creating the reality you want by downloading the playsheets here: www.playsheets.16seconds. co.uk

In the next chapter, Pam will be explaining what beliefs are, how powerful they are and how they can tamper, impact on and if you allow it, sabotage the very thing that you want and the life you want to live.

CHAPTER 4

What Are Beliefs? Are They Facts?

Pam

I recall a conversation with a man I met on a training course prior to doing my coaching and Neuro Linguistic Programme training (NLP) many years ago. He had just finished doing his NLP practitioner training and was so excited about the learning, particularly the part about belief systems and limiting beliefs. I remember (in my ignorance) telling him I didn't have many beliefs (well that was a belief!), that as I'd studied and been through counselling and psychology courses, I was fairly neutral and couldn't think of any beliefs good or otherwise. (Gosh, I did have a lot to learn!) He was really polite and just said, "You'd be surprised how many we have," and then changed the subject.

How ironic that I would later go on to not only find out more about belief systems and how many limiting beliefs I actually had, but love the subject so much it would become my niche in coaching. Through my studying and learning, I've found that finding and changing limiting beliefs for myself, and then later helping others to do the same, was a wonderful way to change my vibration upwards.

I realised early on that if I wanted to achieve my big goals, I'd have to move from a place of fear to a place of courage and that meant it was time to face and work with my fears.

There are two labels for beliefs: **limiting** which hold you back from taking action and **empowering** which move you towards your goal. So how are you to know the difference between a belief and a fact?

Motivational speakers such as Deepak Chopra and Bruce Lipton tell us we have about 70,000 thoughts a day and roughly 95% are negative, redundant or the same as yesterday's. That's a scary thought, isn't it?

So how do we recognise a fact (a thing that is known or proved to be true) as against a limiting belief (a false belief a person acquires as a result of making an incorrect conclusion about something in life)?

For me personally a fact is:

- I currently work as a trainer and coach
- I've had an operation on my foot
- I'm not interested in sport in general

A limiting belief is something that could be changed but I don't believe it can and it stops me achieving my goal:

Scenario 1

- I can't ride a horse
- Q: Do I want to?
- A: Yes

It's a fact with a goal.

Scenario 2

- I can't ride a horse
- Q: Do I want to?
- A: Yes, but I'm not sure I can learn how to

It's a goal with a limiting belief or a limiting belief about being able to learn.

Other limiting beliefs are:

- I'm too old to... could be a limiting belief or other people's beliefs you've bought into. Neuroplasticity[2] and neuroscience[3] are challenging this belief.
- I can't be a success in business because I failed last time – many successful people tried and failed before succeeding.

---

2   Neuroplasticity: The brain's ability to reorganise itself by forming new neural connections throughout life.

3   Neuroscience, also known as Neural Science, is the study of how the nervous system develops, its structure and what it does.

- I can't lose and keep off weight. Sandra has managed to lose and keep off weight for over 15 years! Another two of my friends have lost and kept weight off for 20+ years.

These are limiting beliefs and stories that keep us trapped.

Different beliefs are also held about the Law of Attraction and manifestation. Some people believe that if you dream about something often enough it will eventually appear in your life; others that if you write it down every day for 30 days it will appear, or if you write it out like old-fashioned homework it will appear, or if you struggle and work hard it will appear.

Maybe it will, maybe it won't so we want to debunk some of the myths to help you manifest more of what you want in your life.

Pick a goal

- Write or record your 'story' around this goal

- Notice and get clear about what's a fact versus a limiting belief (beware, your stories **will** contain limiting beliefs dressed up as facts)

- Challenge all limiting beliefs, they send out a negative vibration to the Universe

- What do you allow to limit you?

- Start to notice how you think and what you say

Do you tell yourself the same stories over and over? If you do, ask yourself if you want to keep or change them (more on how to change them in the chapter Changing Beliefs).

Whenever you set a goal, notice your feelings and thoughts. How you feel is everything when it comes to manifesting what you want. Do you feel good thinking about the goal or do you feel negative? Feeling good? The goal resonates with you? Name the feeling. You'll want to recognise it going forward to keep raising your vibration.

You can literally be in any state you want in seconds and any feeling you hold or thought you think for 16 seconds or more kicks in the Law of Attraction and brings you a vibrational match which is the first step towards manifesting what you want.

If you feel uneasy or negative about your goal, name the emotion you're feeling then interrupt it within 16 seconds by changing it to a more positive one. Here's an example:

> "I am feeling X Y Z… and that's OK, I'm being realistic, this feeling is in my energy field so I need to acknowledge it. And now I have, I'd like to feel A B C… instead."

> "What's the first step I could take to move towards feeling ABC?"

Nailing this early on will give you more personal power, awareness and choice.

It's important to mention that this very moment is all that is real. This second that you are reading these words. In a second, this moment will have disappeared and become the past and the next second will become your present. You're on the path to vibrational change when in this state of presence.

I've heard speakers in NLP and mindfulness trainings say people spend too much of their waking time thinking about the past, sometimes with regret, and too much time worrying about the future, forgetting about the present moment, the only thing they have any control over, the only time that is real and where the magic can begin to happen.

To change your vibration and manifest your goals, you need to pay attention to the present moment, how you're feeling, what you're saying and what you're visualising. It may be unrealistic to be mindful and present every second of every day, but you'll reap huge vibrational benefits if you pay some attention to the present moment, as this is where a seed of change can be planted and start to grow.

Doing the above is your first step in recognising the messages and vibrations you are sending to the Universe. Such a simple exercise which can help you spot and change limiting beliefs fast. Limiting beliefs show up in the form of self-talk, they pop into your mind at any given moment. They are sneaky and creep up on you when you're not paying attention. They vibrate negatively and play a part in sabotaging your goals.

It's worth taking a look at the playsheets in the downloadable file for each chapter www.playsheets.16seconds.co.uk which are there to help you make the changes you desire.

Storytelling

> *"I must create a system or be enslaved*
> *by another man's."*
>
> – William Blake

Beliefs are stories you tell yourself over and over. They come from stories you were told when younger as well as personal experiences.

Many will no longer be valid or true and if you let them, they will restrict your thinking and chain you to an unconscious image of who you think you are, thus stopping you from crossing an invisible line of greater success or manifestation.

As adults we repeat our stories over and over to ourselves via our self-talk and then we tell them again, out loud, to family, friends and sometimes even strangers if they're willing to listen. When you do this these stories become your truths, your reality.

Your story, as Sandra mentioned in chapter 1, has a vibration which is similar to a lighthouse sending out a beacon of light to the Universe. It searches for other vibrations that match it which turn up in the form of people, experiences and incidents.

When your vibration finds such a match, bingo! Sympathetic resonance, (which is a harmonic phenomenon wherein a formerly passive string or vibratory body responds to external vibrations to which it has a harmonic likeness), occurs and the two (or more) vibrations start vibrating together in harmony. This provides you with proof that your story is true and factual because you have evidence for it, which may cause you to believe there's nothing you can do to change it, which is a myth.

In such a case, you might think the best thing to do is return to the comfort and ease of what you know, in which case your life will continue as it is, unchallenged. The old story remains your reality, your 'go to', your normal way of thinking. Nothing will change.

These stories were woven into the daily fabric of your life and reinforced when you were very young; they've become your habits and truths and each of these stories has an energetic vibration which attracts like vibrations into your life. They put a cap or ceiling on what you think you can do, be or have. Many stories contain limiting beliefs and negative self-talk, they're emotional states which create highs and lows. They impose limitations, excuses and reasons that stop you stepping into your stretch zone, they keep you stuck and all too often cause you to fall into the victim trap.

Stop for a moment and check if you have an internal voice. Everyone I've met and spoken to about this subject tells me they have some kind of internal self-communication. See if you can find yours. Do you hear a voice, see pictures or feel the words? You can't be wrong. It's your internal communication. Start paying more attention to your inner communication from today and notice what messages it shares with you, and anything unhelpful decide to change.

> *"Your destiny is decided by the choices you make."*
>
> – Tony Robbins

You, like me and others you know, take your stories with you everywhere you go. When you meet people for the first time you tell them your story. If they 'challenge it' by trying to be kind and reassure you it can't be so, of course you're confident, gorgeous, kind or whatever rescuing message they offer, there's a chance you correct them and say, "No, it's like this, it's always been that way," and you recall times and places that prove to them that your story is true. It's called a payoff.

Inspirational personal development speakers such as Tony Robbins, Joe Dispenza and Bruce Lipton say that beliefs create your reality, and in turn the stories you decide to tell yourself and others, and by doing so you reap what you sow and manifest what you're willing to allow into your life.

If you change your beliefs you can change your reality

Please just ponder that for a moment. Could you consider that as a new way to look at your life?

If so, you can learn more about changing beliefs in chapter 7, and if you take a look at the playsheets for chapter 4 exercise (1) it will help you start identifying your limiting beliefs.

Another way to become aware of your story is by taking a brief look at your upbringing (you don't have to delve further than you are comfortable with). Doing this exercise can help you understand where some of your current positive and negative beliefs came from. You'll also find enriching and helpful beliefs as well as out of date or redundant ones.

"A wise man will make more opportunities
than he finds."

– Francis Bacon

Here's my example. My mother came from a poor Irish background, and was the youngest of eight children. They had a very small piece of land to work on and theirs was a tough life. They were brought up to work physically hard, had very little in terms of money or possessions and death was a frequent visitor to their home whilst growing up. My grandfather died when my mother was young, so my grandmother had to cope with feeding eight kids and watch while some of them died as young adults.

My mum left school at 14 to go to work. She was savvy, strong willed, determined and a bit of a rebel. She wanted more for herself (and her future family) than she'd experienced growing up but didn't place a high value on education or tradition to get it. For her it was about hard work and earning money. She and my uncle came to England in the late 1940s.

My dad came from a middle class Irish family of six where they valued education and tradition. His parents weren't wealthy but they managed to send the youngest female child to private school, who went on to become a teacher. Two sisters and a brother went to America where they all did well and my mum's best friend (that's how she met my dad) came to England and met my uncle, a lovely man who is still with us as I write, who had a good job and earned a reasonable living. My dad went on to set up his own business, though he suffered ill health most of my childhood and was in and out of hospital. We four children grew up with very little in terms of objects or money, and there were no government benefits of any type. My mum struggled financially but of course she could handle that as she'd been prepared in childhood and was creative. She managed to get a mortgage, and when we were small we all shared one bedroom as she took in lodgers to pay the bills.

From that snapshot I wonder if you can guess some of the values and beliefs this story passed on to myself and my siblings.

It's worth remembering that the beliefs our parents share with us are impacted by their upbringing, the environment they grew up in, the people they hung out with and their personal experiences.

My life was different from my mum's because of where I lived (London), the decade I was born in where so much had changed for women, the opportunities I had, compared to her, the law regarding the age I had to stay in school until and the fact I could earn my own living. However, the values and beliefs I was given as a child continued to run me unconsciously even though the life I was living was very different from my mum's.

"We are what we repeatedly do."

– Aristotle

Limiting beliefs

We come from our parents, but we are not them. Their belief systems are useful as a benchmark to keep us safe as children, but there comes a time when we need to take ownership of our own lives, become aware of our beliefs, challenge and change those which no longer serve us and create our own.

Here are a few beliefs I was given:

- Life is short

- Life is hard

- You have to work hard to get ahead

- Money doesn't grow on trees

- The world is a dangerous place

- Don't take risks

- Your health is the most important thing you own

- Family is important, be there for each other

- Always be independent

I lived my life by all of these (and more) conscious and unconscious rules (and other ones I'm not going to bore you with) right up until I found coaching and the Law of Attraction. Some I've chosen to keep because they serve me, like 'life is short'. It is, so I choose to:

- recognise, challenge and face my fears
- welcome my mind chatter and get it working for me instead of against me
- take calculated risks
- identify my limiting beliefs such as 'life is hard', and change them into positive affirmations
- stop listening to people who want(ed) to bring me down or stop me growing
- stop playing a small game by stepping into my stretch zone

"Always look for ways to nurture your dreams."

– Lao Tzu

This belief I liked so I decided to keep it: 'you have to work hard to get ahead'. I like working hard, it makes me happy and I do it with ease.

Another one my mum often shared was 'money doesn't grow on trees'; this one created a limiting belief (for me) in terms of what I could 'allow' myself to earn. I know many friends and clients who have a similar unconscious ceiling in place.

Remember my story above, no big money makers in my history, so I had an unconscious financial limitation in place. When I left school, my parents were happy with how much I was earning, had beliefs that 'people with too much money were suspect' and that 'it couldn't buy your health'. So in my mum's eyes I'm doing well, I'm a success, but unconsciously I'm running her story that life is about financial struggle but you survive in spite of it.

So I'm 18 and on track with living my life according to my programming and I'm neither happy nor unhappy at this stage. But if I'm honest, there was something niggling at me, like an itch I couldn't scratch, something saying 'there must be more to my working life than this'. But I wasn't to find out what that really meant for another 22 years.

"The unexamined life is not worth living."

– Plato

From what I share above, is it possible that your 'history' and unconscious programming may be affecting what you will allow into your life? Could it have created the frequency of vibration you are currently operating from? Is it possible it's impacted the choices you made in the past and may continue to make in the future? Is it possible you may not actually have made many choices at all, you may have just run on automatic pilot, carrying forward stories and beliefs from others, who carried them forward from their 'others', with beliefs like, 'it's just the way things are', 'I can't do anything about my lot', 'people like us…'?

Could it be that if you accept others' beliefs and stories about how life 'should' be and don't examine or challenge them, they may shape your current and future reality and what you're manifesting?

To make change happen, you will need to get good at noticing what you say to yourself internally and out loud so you can choose if you want to change it. In the beginning you may need the help of a family member or friend.

"The real voyage of discovery consists not in seeking new landscapes, but in having new eyes."

– Marcel Proust

I used to be an adult teacher in a London college for around 15 years. Initially I taught professional photographic fashion make-up, then teacher training, finally coaching skills. One of the coaching sessions included identifying and changing limiting beliefs where students discussed what limiting beliefs were, how they stopped them achieving goals and the negative feelings and self-fulfilling prophecy they produced. In each of the sessions, my job was to help students discover their negative reality and then introduce them to simple exercises that could change it (I'll share some with you in the downloadable exercises 3, 4 and 5).

The agreement was the students would go away and practise the exercises over the coming week and then report back to the group at the beginning of the following session.

The results were amazing. The testimonials moving, I loved my course, my students and coaching. Having lost it for a while, I now had my purpose back in my work, I had found my calling. My vibration was resonating from a place of joy. And I wasn't even trying to feel this way, I just was. And the floodgates opened in a positive way, my business took off professionally, I was invited to write and deliver the first BTEC coaching course, which was also on offer to other colleges around the UK, and I was told on a regular basis that I was making a difference to people's lives. Only in my dreams (it's a good place to start) could I have felt so fulfilled and it's continued through to today.

Training to be a coach[4] put me on the Law of Attraction positive vibrational map. It helped me to start thinking about what I wanted instead of what I didn't want. It highlighted my limiting beliefs so I could choose to challenge and change them and it opened my eyes to new opportunities which I started saying yes to, that previously I would have ignored or shied away from.

Beliefs and vibrations

Beliefs show up in your mind chatter, actions and non-actions. Start noticing how you and others repeat stories about particular goals over and over again. Notice how convincing your stories, both positive and negative, are and how easy it is to call them facts. No doubt you'll have endless evidence to prove they're true. Negative beliefs are powerful, controlling, hypnotic, sometimes depressing and can even be dangerous.

In coaching sessions, many of my clients discover unhelpful, out of date beliefs are still running their lives. This realisation helps them become conscious of how they've been trapped in an old story which can now be changed.

A simple exercise to help you become aware is to have someone you trust reflect your language back to you word for word when you're being negative, so you can hear your limiting beliefs. This awareness gives you choice to do something or nothing about it.

---

4   The coaching process involves asking a client what they want to achieve in an area of their life, setting a goal, breaking the goal down into manageable steps, selecting one step and making it into a specific goal, asking the client open questions to enable them find their own answers so they can choose to take regular and consistent action towards its fulfilment.

Believing is seeing

As mentioned, beliefs create and shape your reality. The frequency at which they vibrate attracts more of the same. They determine what you expect and what you'll manifest from the Universe.

Many people I get to work with are dissatisfied with an area or two of their lives, they move through life, often at a fast pace, on automatic pilot, not noticing what they think, what's important to them, what they believe or what they want. They subconsciously accept and believe they can only have what they're currently experiencing even though they consciously want something different. This is their psychological baseline.

We all have a psychological baseline, it's that ceiling I mentioned previously. The psychology courses I've attended suggest it's set in childhood based on messages and experiences you've received. It can be changed, but it takes awareness, time, mindfulness and practice.

Changing limiting beliefs takes time. I know, it may not be what you wanted to hear because another myth is 'if I think hard enough about what I want, I should be able to have it now!' If you can buy it on Amazon that may be true, for as one of my coaches said, "The reason Prime is so popular is because we can have what we want (from the Amazon store) pretty much now!" Life is a little bit different, things take time to grow, but with a little bit of effort and practice you can start ordering from the universal store and they will arrive at exactly the right time, but the order needs to be from an authentic place of surrender and allowing.

Beliefs are emotional and some of your daily emotions and reactions are more suited to you being two or three years old rather than the adult you have grown into – well in terms of years anyway. I say that because I don't know anyone who was taught how to emotionally or mentally be a 'grown up'. I, and most people I know, were told to 'grow up' because of being a certain age.

However, if your childhood lower vibrations, such as anger, disappointment or frustration, haven't been recognised and worked through, they may be driving your everyday reactions to situations. It's worth considering, because as you already know, if you're subconsciously vibrating at a lower level but your conscious goal requires a higher level, the subconscious will win.

In the chapter Who You Are Physically, I mentioned David Hawkins, who created the Map of Consciousness, where he calibrated each emotion on a vibrational scale. He says that everything has an energy vibration – thoughts, things, people, places, emotions; quantum physics is saying the same using different language.

He says we attract like frequencies into our lives, which as you know means you'll attract people, opportunities and things that are vibrating at the same frequency as yourself into your life, even though you don't consciously want them (it's called chemistry in relationships). Whether you believe his research or not, it's worth considering it if you want to improve what you are manifesting.

If we take the emotion of fear, it vibrates at 100 on Hawkins' scale[5]. It causes us pain as do all the emotions that vibrate below 200. According to Hawkins, positive change occurs at level 200, which is the vibration of courage. Here, he says, there is an awareness that thoughts and actions influence reality.

---

5   On a scale of 1 to 1,000 with 1 being the lowest level of truth and consciousness and 1,000 being the highest level of truth and consciousness.

So let's say that your unconscious baseline is fear (mine was), but your conscious goal is to work in a joyful environment making a difference to both your own and others' lives (joy vibrates at 540). Can you start to see there's a bit of a problem regarding the conscious and unconscious demands on your goal and how being misaligned could be a problem?

Here's an example: you choose to set a goal to leave your negative job in a negative environment (I did) and start planning to manifest a positive environment to work in. To move towards the goal, you might choose to create a vision board or regularly daydream about it, perhaps you'll write a story or draw a picture of it, or reflect or make a plan.

If one of the above resonated with you, you may find the first step is easy. But what's the next step? What will it involve? What action will you need to take? What will you need to do that's different from before? What could you try that you haven't tried before? What could you do that is new that could stretch you?

How do you feel about taking a different action? Unsure? Scared? After all, you've heard the saying 'better the devil you know'. What will you do if your mind chatter kicks in and tells you it's best to be safe and not rock the boat, you have a lot to lose if you step up and do something new, I mean, what will others think of you? What might you risk or lose? You don't know what it feels like to work in a place where it's positive or joyful so how will you recognise it?

Can you see how easy it could be to start to doubt yourself and the idea of the new goal? Maybe you'll talk yourself out of taking any action by telling yourself such environments don't exist. Or if they do you won't be able to keep up the positive attitude, you've got experience from the past that shows it's easier to be negative, and you know when you look at your story it's true for most, if not all of your life. Negativity is what you know, it's what you're good at, it's normal, so why bother trying to change?

Even though it's painful to live in a place of fear, for many of us it's comfortable and you may have a belief that it's safer to stay with the familiar than to risk failing trying something new that you don't really believe in.

At fear you're vibrating at level 100. If your goal is at level 540 no wonder you'll give up, the leap is too far up the ladder, literally as well as energetically, and if you didn't know about emotional vibrations before maybe now you can see why the Law of Attraction wasn't working for you. But as Sandra previously mentioned, the Law of Attraction is always working for you, it's giving you what you vibrate at.

It's great to know you can change your reality and your future by setting goals in line with your vibrational level. It made me very happy, but you do need a little patience and courage and these were two qualities and vibrations that historically I didn't have. So guess what you do next? You set a goal. What do you want? It doesn't matter if you've failed in the past, you know more now.

As William James, a pioneering American psychologist and philosopher, said, "Success of goals means avoiding pretensions and failure by adopting less ambitious goals." By doing this you'll build your self-belief and confidence.

By taking the first step towards your goal and seeing a small win you are working with the real emotional vibration you are operating at. When you succeed, your body will release the feel good hormone dopamine as a reward. This causes you to want more of the good feeling, so you take another small step, you get rewarded again, so you take another. And before you know it time has passed, your vibration has shifted upwards and the goal you set is becoming easier to believe in.

There is a saying 'seeing is believing', I prefer the saying: **'believing is seeing'**. In NLP I was taught that there are millions of bits of information floating around both inside and outside of us but consciously we can only focus on 7-9 bits at any time. I mention this because in your life you will be looking for and seeking out those 7-9 bits which conform with your belief system.

If you want to understand more about this, you might like to read about the Reticular Activating System (RAS). It's situated at the base of the brain above the spine. All the information you're presented with every day is evaluated through the 'eyes' of the RAS. It determines what gets through. The idea is that the RAS behaves like an unconscious heat-seeking missile looking for its target which is driven by your (subconscious) values and beliefs. Once something is brought to its attention consciously as well as subconsciously, the RAS will notice and pay attention to it for as long as it remains important. This is why you've manifested what you currently have in your career, finances, relationship, confidence, etc.

Below, I'm going to tell you a simple story to give you an idea of how the RAS works on a subconscious level and why it's important to know about it, as your childhood programming (ie values and beliefs) is causing your RAS to seek out what it thinks is good for you and therefore what it will allow you to manifest. Awareness of it will give you more choice from now on.

I also want you to realise that anything which has been programmed in childhood (ie values and beliefs) will subconsciously cause your RAS to drive your behaviour, habits and actions throughout your life in relation to what you can and can't have.

If you want to see a great YouTube example of this, take a look at Dave's Brain, episode 1 by John Assaraf a behaviour expert. It's three minutes long and I love it.

So here's a personal example to highlight the above, and after you've read it, go and test it for yourself.

My husband and I were going to an event in London but were a bit early. We were right by Selfridges so we popped in to take a look around the fashion department. I love shopping and can spend hours wandering around looking at lovely things and I don't have to buy anything to get pleasure from it, though I do like buying too!

So we were looking at different brands and there was one we came across that he hadn't heard of before. I was a little surprised because he knows a lot about everything. The moment passed. We walked around a bit more and then went outside. As we waited to cross the road a bus passed us with a huge advertisement for this very designer. "Look," I said, "there's that designer again!" (we'd never have noticed it under normal circumstances as it would just have been a bus with an advert on it).

We got to the event early, as always with my husband, and I was flicking through a magazine and guess what? There was a full-page advert for that designer which I showed him. There were full-page adverts for many other designers too but I didn't concentrate or fix on them because we'd had a conversation about just that one and I had been slightly surprised so my mind was now focused on it subconsciously as well as consciously.

Do you see what I mean? When you aim for something, look for something, set a goal, know what you want (or don't want), your RAS starts putting it into your 7-9 bits of conscious focus and you will keep seeing or hearing about it until you decide to take action and seek it out properly. If the goal fits with your beliefs about yourself and your vibration matches its vibration, you'll probably be successful in achieving it with ease.

Alternatively, if it doesn't fit with how you see yourself, because it's way above what you believe you deserve, are worthy of or will allow into your life, and the vibration of what you want doesn't match the vibration of your emotion around the goal, your mind chatter might intervene and tell you why you can't have it or why it's not important to have it. Back to safety island, comfort zone, feeling stuck and living a mediocre life.

And, as you already know from what you've read and watching the YouTube video, this happens because you have unconscious programming which silently runs in the background and affects the decisions or actions it will allow you to take.

When I understood this vibration gap, which you can read more about in chapter 5, I set a goal to become more courageous. The first thing I had to do was get clear about what courage meant to me around my career goal. So I did a mind map. Next I put in order, the steps that needed to be taken, starting with the easiest which was the least scary, so I could match my real vibration with the actions that needed to be taken. In doing this, it helped me with my second goal, developing patience. To this day I still have to work with being patient, I do pretty well and forgive myself when I slip up; after all, I am human.

MYTH DEBUNK: All you need to do is create a vision board or think about your goal each day.

MANIFESTATION METHOD: Programme your RAS by visualising, thinking and *feeling* into what you want and taking regular action.

So to start manifesting more of what you want, become aware of the beliefs you hold about yourself and your goals. Challenge them by replacing them with new positive beliefs.

Practise reinforcing the new beliefs until you believe them and notice how the Universe brings you more of what you want and it all starts with focusing for 16 seconds.

Enjoy practising. You can download your playsheets here: www.playsheets.16seconds.co.uk

The next chapter will explain how you can close the all-important vibrational gap between what you desire and where you currently stand in relation to getting what you want.

CHAPTER 5

Bridging The Gap From Where You Are Now To Where You Want To Be

Sandra

I'm hoping from what you have read so far that you are beginning to believe that you can create your own reality and understand what can either stop you or support you in doing so.

As we have previously touched on, the length of time before you achieve what it is you want to be, do or have is dependent on how far away or how close you are to really *knowing* (not just believing) that you are, at your present moment in time, creating and manifesting it into your reality. This length of time is known as the gap.

The gap

The gap is where many of us exist most of the time. We have desires and as we have explained earlier, our limiting beliefs in achieving what we want are far removed from the vibration or energy of the desire. So you develop an all-important vibrational gap between your desire and the belief of ever having whatever it is you want to manifest.

So, think about something that you want – do you think mostly of what you want or do you focus more on the not having it? Are you focusing more on your current reality where it is showing you that what you want still hasn't manifested? You're in debt and you have outstanding bills to pay, but the windfall or the wage rise that you're hoping for still hasn't happened. Where is your dominant focus – on the unpaid bills or the windfall that you're hoping to manifest? And more importantly, which reality do you believe in? The unpaid bills that you are giving focus to or the windfall that you are hoping for but hasn't yet appeared in the here and now that you are living?

And this is the crucial question. Do you believe that you can have what you want? If your thoughts are regularly turning to 'Where is it?' 'When will I have it? 'How will I get it? 'It's not here yet', it's extremely likely that you're feeling disbelief that what you want will ever turn up. And when you keep noticing what you want isn't showing up, how do you feel? It's likely to be a range of emotions such as, worry, frustration, fear, disbelief and despondency. But to sum it up, you're not feeling very good!

Now once again, imagine what you do want and ask yourself *why* do you want it? As Abraham-Hicks teaches, most of us want what we want because we think we'll feel good in the having of it. Think about that for a minute. Whatever desire you have right now, you believe you will feel better or happier when you have it. So, if we understand and now believe that we have to be a vibrational match to what we want, we have to find a way to feel good even if our desire hasn't yet showed up. The emotions you may feel when thinking about your current 'difficult reality' (despondent, worried, anxious etc) are poles apart from the vibrational match of excitement and happiness when thinking about what you do want.

So what can help you to bridge the gap and bring you closer to being in the vibrational vicinity of the very thing that you want, but just the thought of it and the fear of not having it is keeping you in the manifesting gap that you have created? We need to soothe your resistance around the belief that you haven't yet received what it is you want and support you in moving from the unhappy, resistant emotions mentioned above to higher flying, easier feeling, allowing emotions.

Let's look at some methods that you can choose to adopt which will help you to feel good about the very thing you want and don't yet have, thereby closing the gap and becoming the manifestor of your dreams.

More about your emotional guidance system

So, this is where our emotional guidance system is all-important. As we've already mentioned, your emotions are key indicators as to where you are standing right at this moment in relation to what it is you desire. Any resistant (bad feeling) emotion keeps you at a distance from being a vibrational match to what you want. So, as I've just said and will keep repeating due to its fundamental importance, you want what you want because you think you'll be happier for the having of it. So when you're feeling an emotion that doesn't feel good, you are not in the vicinity of attracting what you want. Do you remember a game that we used to play when we were children about trying to find something that was hidden and the closer we got, we would be told 'you're getting warmer' and then as we moved away, we would be told 'you're getting cooler'? When you're not feeling good and in resistance, you're not only getting cooler, you're stone cold!

In Pam's chapters Who You Are Physically and What Are Beliefs, she mentions David Hawkins' emotional scale and his logarithmic progression scale to measure each emotional state and how it affects what you manifest.

Abraham-Hicks also teaches about the importance of our emotions and the influence they have on what we're attracting at any moment depending on where we are on the emotional scale as listed below. As Abraham-Hicks stated in their book *Ask and It's Given*, our emotions range from the high-flying feelings of joy, appreciation and love, down to fear, grief and powerlessness etc.

1. Joy/Appreciation/Empowered/Freedom/Love

2. Passion

3. Enthusiasm/Eagerness/Happiness

4. Positive Expectation/Belief

5. Optimism

6. Hopefulness

7. Contentment

8. Boredom

9. Pessimism

10. Frustration/Irritation/Impatience

11. Overwhelm

12. Disappointment

13. Doubt

14. Worry

15. Blame

16. Discouragement

17. Anger

18. Revenge

19. Hatred/Rage

20. Jealousy

21. Insecurity/Guilt/Unworthiness

22. Fear/Grief/Depression/Despair/Powerlessness

When we are feeling the upper end emotions, we are feeling good, easy and in the flow of life and because we feel that way, we are more of a vibrational match to the very thing that we want (remember that we want our desire because we think we will feel good in the having of it). We are getting warmer and warmer.

However, when we are experiencing the lower end of the emotions, we are getting cooler and cooler and we are moving away from being a vibrational match to what feels good (unfortunately, we can easily experience those lower end emotions if we really want or need something and it appears it's not coming into our physical reality any time soon). ***We can't hope that with feeling bad, we can still manifest the very thing that we think will help us to feel good.*** I really want you to read that sentence again and take it in, because many of us will *try to feel good* about the very thing we want not yet showing up, or our life not feeling great, but the impatient, disappointed emotional energy you're *really* feeling and emanating will always be your true signpost of what you're attracting (which is more of the stuff that is making life tricky).

But how do we get to feel anywhere near the top of the emotional scale when we are residing somewhere near the middle or indeed the bottom? It would be very unusual to be able to take a single leap from one end of the scale to the other, so as Pam mentioned in relation to setting goals, incremental steps are the key to moving up the emotional ladder and feeling better and therefore more in sync and closer to a good feeling. As you can see from the above emotional scale, anger is higher up the ladder than fear or grief, and frustration or impatience is higher than worry. So, it's not about beating yourself up if you're not feeling like you can jump for the moon, but it's about gently reaching for that better feeling thought, step by step, moment by moment.

You probably want to shout at me, "If I could get to a better feeling thought about my situation or what I want and the fact that it's not here yet, then don't you think I would?!" The problem with trying to feel good about something you feel bad about is the momentum you have now built on the disbelief around ever getting what you want. Your predominant thoughts will be focused on what's currently happening, not on moving towards the outcome you want.

The gap remains when your dominant focus is on the situation that caused you to want something different. As we have mentioned before, we tend to give more attention and therefore more credence to the current 'reality' that we are living. We believe that as we are living it, so it is and our attention to it attracts more of what we're living. So if you want a fulfilling, loving relationship, it is likely you are thinking more about the pattern of previous relationships that didn't work out too good. This may have included thoughts of how you compromised yourself, instead of heading your thoughts towards the unconditional love that could be flowing to you if you were able to feel and think a slightly better feeling thought.

If you are unwell and you want wellness, it is likely that you are thinking about the cause of your unwellness, rather than a better feeling thought that could lift you slightly up the emotional scale towards feeling more at peace with your situation and therefore allowing the cells of your body to do their inherent and natural job of moving into wellbeing. You get the gist.

So, when you focus on a reality you don't want, the gap between where you currently stand and what you want remains open. So what is the answer? How do you find an easier way of closing that gap? One of the ways is distraction! And how do you distract when you're in the throes of focusing on what appears to be going wrong? Change the subject of your focus. Don't try and change how you feel about what isn't good in your life right now. The feeling you have about it has built momentum and is strong in its attracting more of what you don't want if you keep giving it thought and attention. So instead, focus on any subject where you can incrementally move up the emotional scale towards appreciation and satisfaction.

Appreciation and satisfaction

How does the word satisfaction make you feel? So so? A bit blah? A great place to be in? Wanting more? To close the vibrational gap from where you are to where you want to be, your sweet spot is to find satisfaction where you are and eager for more. Satisfied with the small things as well as satisfied with the big things in your life. Acknowledging that it doesn't always have to be champagne corks popping but a steady lining up of the small things for you to look at and know 'I created that' and feeling the sense of satisfaction as each one presents itself. The satisfaction of a job well done (whatever that means for you); a fun time with a friend; your day unfolding just as you envisaged and knowing that with this good, momentum building feeling of seeing things work out, you create even more satisfying moments.

This recently happened to me. I was on my way back home from a wonderful day's training in the city and I was meeting my husband for dinner in a restaurant close to where we live. I knew that the Underground system was having problems, but I also knew that if I was going to take what appeared to be the easier option of taking an overground train to where I live, I would be waiting quite a while for connections. I knew I could be home in a much shorter time if I travelled by the Underground tube system, but this 'depended' on the Underground system working well!

So, before I started off on my travels, already with an easy, flowing vibrational attitude from the day I had intended and experienced, I had a very clear intention that my travels home on the Underground would be seamless and it would all flow. I wasn't buying into the so-called 'reality' that was showing up on the latest travel update. I knew what I wanted and decided consciously to create it by setting an intention and knowing the creation of it was perfectly possible.

And needless to say, not only did it all perfectly just weave together, but I also arrived much earlier than I had thought. So much earlier in fact that I was waiting for my husband for 15 minutes! I used that time to feel the wonderful emotion of satisfaction, knowing that I created that joyful experience from a clear intention and a belief that I could choose and create the reality I wanted. There was no resistance within me concerning my journey home and I closed my vibrational gap literally from what the 'reality' appeared to be to how I wanted it to play out. Very satisfying and I'm eager for more!

With everything wonderful that you have created, do you stop and feel a sense of appreciation? Do you feel into your blessings? Do you allow time to just stop for a moment and feel your emotions moving up the emotional scale as you appreciate? Can you imagine how your day can build from a platform of appreciation into a day of full-blown joy, where every intention you have put out from this basis flows effortlessly to you and around you?

Every morning I have a process where I allow myself the time to begin my day coming from a sense of appreciation. I write my appreciation journal, appreciate my surroundings noticing how my emotions are stable towards the top end of the emotional scale. From this place of feeling good, I then stretch out on my yoga mat and give my physical body the gift of stretching and strengthening. I am now on my high-flying disc, satisfied where I am, appreciating blessings, attracting more of them and ready for the most wonderful day ahead. There is then no gap between me and the connected part of me.

This for me is a time that's sacrosanct. It's protected. It's unusual for me to speak to a client very early on in the morning as my process comes first and then I am the best I can be for myself and my clients and the day that follows. Needless to say, on the few days where I have an earlier start, I will make sure that I am awake even earlier to experience the joy of my morning process and set my vibrational set point for the day – a set point of satisfaction, appreciation and excited anticipation for the day ahead.

Feeling appreciative is a practice that will really serve to nudge you up the emotional scale. However, our usual practice as human beings is to stop appreciating when experiences turn up that are challenging. We become all consumed with what is happening around us, in free fall to the lower end of the emotional scale, aware that we don't feel good but doing nothing to stop the momentum and we allow any feelings of appreciation or satisfaction to leave us until the 'crisis' is over and we remember we want to feel good. We then begin the morning process once more. Of course, this is OK. But it's important to remember that we always have a choice – do I want to feel good as much as I can with the conditions around me or do I want to allow the situation to consume me and feel the gloom of the 'reality' around me?

However bad it is (and I do acknowledge that there are times of grief and sadness where this may not be possible, at least for a while), we *can* make a decision to feel good. We *can* make the choice to focus on satisfaction and appreciation however fleeting the thoughts may be. Each thought is a chink in the darkness and heads you towards the light where you can experience relief and close the gap. Even when you are not feeling good, appreciate your emotional guidance system for making you aware of how you are feeling so that you can choose in that moment of awareness the direction in which to go. We can truly appreciate even the smallest of things if we have an intention to do so.

Feel it and see it

As we've written in an earlier chapter, visualising supports the manifestation of what you want. But seeing and *feeling* into what you want helps to close the gap from where you are in relation to what you want and standing in the vibrational place of receiving. Remember, this gap is energetic; it's vibrational. So you want to be closing the energetic gap that is between you and what you want. As we know, we identify differently with our learning skills. We tend to be visual (connecting more easily to what we see), auditory (to what we hear – certain music or songs for instance can trigger an emotional response for some people) or kinaesthetic (more of a hands-on way to learn and feeling the emotions of what we're focusing on). To close the gap, you need to see, hear and feel what you want to create.

If you can visualise what you want and don't feel it, the connection to what you want isn't as strong as when you emotionally and physically connect with the whole complete image of what you want to create. As you stand in the vision of your intended creation and see and hear what is going on within this vision and feel into what it feels like to have created it exactly as you want it, you have become one with what you want and you have closed the vibrational gap, putting out to the Universe a frequency of a completed desire and thereby (as like attracts like) bringing the manifested form quickly to you.

I would love for you to do this exercise every time you think about what it is you want:

- Take a few moments in a quiet space with your eyes closed, thinking about what it is you want.

- In your mind's eye, see it in a way that it is already manifested as you want it.

- As you see your creation in your mind's eye, notice the sounds you hear in this vision, any voices that may be speaking, hands that may be clapping.

- Notice the colours that you see in this vision within your mind's eye. Make those colours brighter and bolder. Increase the size of this picture.

- Now, as you stand with this bright, clear, big and bold vision in your mind's eye, feel how you feel in the vision. Feel the exhilaration of everything happening around you as you want it. The feeling of fun as you can see yourself in the creating process. The feeling of joy, as you are enjoying the fruits of what you have created in this vision. Make those feelings stronger until the vision and the feelings make you want to run around your home with your arms in the air, shouting 'Yes! Yes! Yes!' You have now closed any gap and you have become one with your completed vibrational manifestation, joyfully living life while the physical manifestation catches up (which is literally around the corner).

Please practise this. Have fun with it. Feel how good it feels to have it – vibrationally at first and then in your physical manifested reality. Remember, you want what you want because you think you will feel good in the having of it. And as you now know, everything that is manifested in the physical has to be initially vibrational. And so in doing this exercise not only are you feeling good, you are also allowing the vibrational reality to emit out into the Universe at the same time. A win-win!

Relax and detach from the outcome

There is however a caveat to the above process and one that is all-important in closing the vibrational gap. As I explained when detailing the Law of Detachment, trusting that you have asked and it is given, even if you can't immediately see it showing up in your physical reality, means that you will be more capable of letting go and detaching from the outcome. You can then go about your business of appreciating. Letting go and detaching is crucial. If you don't let go after being clear with your desire, you will be looking for evidence of it showing up and once again your focus will quickly shift to the 'not yet having it'. You are then back in the cycle of building the momentum of lack, of thinking and feeling impatient, frustrated and disappointed (way down the emotional scale).

As we have already said, the universal energies are all around you, ready to pick up on the signal that you are emanating. As you relax, you allow. As you stress, you resist. It really is that simple. As you relax and trust in the knowledge that you have asked and that the co-operative components are lining up for you thanks to the Law of Attraction feeling no resistance from you to what you want, you can feel the connection to all that you are – the creator that you came here to be. Tap into the power that is you – desiring, asking and allowing the creation of what you want and joyfully feel into this expansion. This is what you came here for and relaxing into this state enables a closing of the gap.

Comparison

We now know that resistance (lower end feeling emotions) keeps us in the vibrational gap. And in my experience with helping thousands of people, comparison to others with what we look like, what we have, our work, our homes, our cars, where we go on holiday, even our family and friendships can lead to not feeling enough or not having enough. We then look for what we believe we don't have and it certainly doesn't feel good. But even more importantly, when you feel this way, you separate yourself from who you truly are. You separate from your inner being – that wise part of you (the largest part of you) who comes from love, abundance, the joy in satisfaction and stands happily waiting for you to come into alignment to all of those good feeling emotions. And this you can do when you're focused on appreciating what you do have and moving with the dance of life, despite the conditions of what may be going on that could sway you from your centred place of peace.

But you also live with an onslaught of media, social media, television, advertising, celebrity, expectations and subliminal messages of what you should have and how you should be living. A recent study by the University of Houston and published in the *Journal of Social and Clinical Psychology* found that the amount of time spent on Facebook comparing oneself to others can be linked to the causes of depression. As researcher Mai-Ly Steers stated: "It doesn't mean Facebook causes depression, but that depressed feelings and lots of time on Facebook and comparing oneself to others tend to go hand in hand."

As we know, most posts that are put on any social media platform tend to be posted when something good is happening – a holiday, a wonderful party, an achievement – images of a life that appears to be amazing. But the tendency then seems to lead to a comparison of your life to theirs and usually you tend to think that your life falls short. But what is the 'reality' of what's going on? Everyone has moments of joy and moments of being thrown off by different forms of turmoil, but that's forgotten when you are seeing these isolated images of this great life that you feel is so much better than your own.

Don't get me wrong. I want everyone to be living a wonderful life. But as we have said before, we are on this planet to evolve and grow and we sometimes have huge spurts of growth from an experience that doesn't feel that great in the moment it's happening. We all experience these moments, but we tend not to plaster them all over social media. So what we see reported on the social platforms is not a true representation of what is fully going on. So you end up comparing your life to a small proportion of someone else's. It doesn't add up. Could we (with absolutely no judgment) call that madness? Ideally, to close that gap, we want to stay centred in our own alignment regardless of what we read and hear.

Stay aligned with your inner being and don't take the vibrational hit!

So, what does that mean, 'don't take the vibrational hit'? To close the vibrational gap from where you are to what you desire, it's necessary to feel good, satisfied, happy, at ease, aligned – you choose whatever word describes your feeling good state. But, as humans, we have a habit of thinking we'll be helpful and be the sponge or the battering ram for anyone who needs to offload whatever is negatively affecting them. We are happy to be the sacrificial recipient so that others can feel better. But by doing that you are willingly moving into a resistant energy that will widen the gap from where you are to what you want.

I have a client who I coach from a vibrational perspective of alignment and in one of our recent sessions, she mentioned that when on a recent long car trip with her partner to a party they were attending, she thought she would 'allow' her partner to speak about his ex and the trauma that is going on. She was feeling guilty that she had put boundaries to protect her energy state when he quite clearly wanted to talk about it and offload. As he started to speak about the situation, they both became very down, very heavy and repeated the same conversation they have had every single time they have spoken about the same subject with no solution.

They continued to make their way to the party in a very depressed way, until she thought of the idea of asking him what his favourite song is. They sang the song and others as a duet and the energy started to lift and they were once more back on track for an enjoyable journey and a fun party. But by thinking she *should* let him offload as she hadn't done that for a while, she took the vibrational hit. This meant neither of them felt good for a long part of the journey – certainly at the cool end of getting what she wants (an easy, loving, fun relationship) and she then also took on the effort and hard work of getting them both back up the emotional scale.

So why do you disconnect from yourself and run from happiness and your own vibrational alignment? Because you have developed a habit of sacrificing how happy you are to try and raise other people's emotions, when they have already built momentum for themselves on the lower end of the emotional scale. As I have mentioned in chapter 1, we cannot help anyone from this place of lowering our vibration to match where someone else is. You just add to the momentum of the lower feeling emotions. As you saw from my client's example, she recognised she had moved from a happy place into a heavy, dark place and chose very quickly to not stay there. As a result, she had to work to support her partner up the vibrational scale, which (thankfully) he was obviously ready for or they would have both entered the party in a very resistant state and the momentum of unhappiness would have built.

The only way you can truly help anyone is to stay centred in your alignment – looking for solutions, not problem focused. Trusting that all is happening perfectly, not 'why me?' Choosing to appreciate and not look for examples in your life of how 'bad' it is. From this better-feeling perspective, you can see more of the bigger picture, focus with clarity and not take the vibrational hit. A solution in the example I've offered may be that my client's partner seeks out a more appropriate professional to speak to. She can then focus on being loving, supportive and feeling good – a perfect way of true help – coming from an aligned place and no vibrational gap between her and all of who she truly is.

Giving as opposed to getting

This wisdom comes from His Holiness the Dalai Lama. When we think about what we want, there is no quicker way to close the vibrational gap than giving, and giving from a place of joy. Not giving because you think you'll get what you want more rapidly and not giving because you feel obligated (remember, when you feel obligated or come from a place of 'should', you are not aligned with who you truly are). There is absolutely nothing to say that you have to give to everyone who asks you for money and it is truly OK to give yourself permission to say no if it doesn't feel right to you. Once again, this is where your emotional guidance system is helping to guide you and when you override that guidance by acting on *should*, you can feel the discord within you.

When you are coming from a place of ease, joy and pleasure in the giving, it feels good and you're aligned. There is no gap between you and you. It feels wonderful. You don't even think of any consequence, it just feels right and all is well. And when you are thinking of giving as opposed to getting, you are not focused on the lack of what you have. Think about this. Generally, when you focus on getting, it's because you believe you don't have enough of what it is you want and then you open up the vibrational gap and you are moving from the 'hotter' to the 'cooler' place in relation to what you want to be, do or have. Focus on the joy of giving from a place within that feels good, authentic and connected, and like a miracle, you will be attracting the very thing that you want to create. You have closed the vibrational gap.

Be kind to yourself

One way that vibrational gap will remain wide open is to read this, practise and then beat yourself up when you go back into an old habit of disconnecting and coming from the human part of you (the ego). Please be kind to yourself. You are changing habits that you have developed for many years, and the Lizard part of the brain which is responsible for processing our emotions, will use every trick in the book to keep you doing exactly what you have always done to keep you 'safe'.

And not to forget, the momentum of the Law of Attraction is also giving you more of what you're thinking and feeling. Pam and I are writing this book to make you aware that you're not weak, it's not about willpower. It's about how the brain will either support or sabotage you hand in hand with the vibrational Law of Attraction and the universal laws. We want you to have this knowledge and take small steps towards a new way of thinking, believing and behaving. A way that will not only close the vibrational gap, but also lead you away from a life of mediocrity to a life of absolute joy, ease and wonderful creation.

MYTH DEBUNK: If you want something and you focus your thoughts on it, you will magically receive it.

MANIFESTATION METHOD: When you have a desire, check in with what you are actually focusing on. Are you focusing on what you want or the reason why you want it – debt, lack, fear? Focus enough to put your attention only on what you **do** want, as no manifestation can happen when you are muddying your vibrational point of attraction by thinking about the current situation that's causing the desire.

Download the playsheets here: www.playsheets.16seconds.co.uk to support you with short exercises to bridge the gap from where you currently stand and move you closer to what you want.

In the next chapter, Pam will guide you to also bridge the gap by showing you *how* you can change those limiting thoughts and beliefs that are keeping you stuck and preventing you from moving forward into all of who you are.

CHAPTER 6

Changing Beliefs

"Reality is merely an illusion,
albeit a very persistent one."

– Albert Einstein

Pam

When reading a personal development book I've noticed that if there are too many suggestions on offer from the author that I have to follow in order to make the difference I desire, I don't tend to do any of them. I might like and want to do them all, but I don't. Do you? What I do is pick one or two to focus on and practise them over and over until I see some change.

I think personal development books are great. They give us ideas and information we may or may not know, they sometimes confirm what we do know, they give us other people's stories which may motivate and inspire us. Sometimes we just don't agree with the tips or we've tried them and they didn't work for us, but at the end of the book, as much as we've enjoyed reading it, we may not do anything at all.

If the above resonates with you, and you might not do any of the things we offer you, that this is just another book you're going to read hoping change will magically happen, stop now and ask yourself: what are you going to do differently this time?

Consider making some notes as you go through this chapter.

When people write books, they write from their perspective, their world, what worked for them, but that doesn't mean it will work for you. Your neurons, your internal processors may fire and work in a different sequence, so our intention has been to share our stories and things that have and haven't worked for us but have worked for clients, so you have a variety of tips to choose from, all the while remembering you only need to pick one or two that you like.

I was working with a long-standing client yesterday; she knows a lot about personal development. She said she has a well-balanced life, apart from one area. I noticed her voice and energy were heavy and slightly negative when she spoke of her goal. She shared all the things she had done to achieve this goal, without success. She'd done a lot. I asked her to tell me all the things she hadn't yet tried for different reasons that might improve this area. There were quite a few.

She told me how each day she stepped into the goal and tried to 'feel it', she said positive affirmations but struggled with visualising and knew she 'should' work on that. She was struggling with visualising it. I know her preferred learning style is feeling and auditory, so I asked her, "Who says you have to visualise it?" She paused and said, "Good point, maybe I don't," and from that she came up with a different approach. One of her ideas made her laugh, the energy shifted, she felt lighter about the goal, the vibration had changed, she now looked forward to working on it her way.

You see she was working so hard on the goal, trying to throw everything at it, that the energy flowing towards the goal resonated at a vibration of effort, frustration, negativity and heaviness. She'd read, or been told, that visualisation is essential to achieving a goal. Maybe it is if you have a preference for visual learning styles, not everyone does, but that doesn't mean you can't 'try' and visualise; in fact, if you can describe something you are visualising it.

Anyway, because my client was following someone else's 'order of rules', she thought if she didn't do everything she 'should' do, according to other people, she wouldn't be successful at achieving the goal. Thing is, she'd been trying to achieve it for years without success, doing it the way other people said she should and it hadn't worked, but now she's found her way, maybe it will.

That's good news, because you don't have to do all of the things we offer you (you don't have to do any of them). You just need to consider doing one, over and over again, because as Mark Waldham, neuroscientist and coach says, "What you consistently practise creates automaticity," and Joe Dispenza on one of his YouTube videos shows how through conscious focus it is possible to step into the field of potentiality, and we will learn more from the next chapter on Creating your Reality how important focus is.

Take a moment right now and think about anything you've ever changed in your life.

What made that change happen?

Was it desire? Skill set? Decision? Pain? Pleasure? What?

Write about it now if you can and then hold that knowledge in your thought field as you read this chapter.

You already know you only need one technique that works for you to make change happen. For me, past and present, it's positive affirmations. Even though they're old school they work for me.

For you they might not work so I'm going to bring you other ideas in this chapter. Please find one that works for you, or after reading the chapter come up with your own ideas and then take gentle action on it, without any attachment to the outcome. If you need a reminder, re-read the chapter on the universal laws.

"Logic will get you from A to B,
imagination will take you everywhere."
– Albert Einstein

If like me you are interested in history, it doesn't take much investigation to realise that pretty much everything you see around you once didn't exist. It started as an idea in someone's mind, it wasn't real, it was just a thought, an idea, a picture or a flash of inspiration, it became real because there was a desire to make it so.

The following were ridiculed or considered faddish:

• Thomas Edison and the light bulb

- Bicycles – a hot fad in 1890
- The motor car – impractical in 1902

What about the telephone, how crazy was that idea? And don't get me started on mobile phones, who could have imagined how small they would become and how much information they would be able to access, it still blows my mind.

What about the internet and airplanes and 3D imaging? I could go on but I'm sure you get the idea.

So it's important for you to remember as we look at ways to implement changing beliefs that people, ideas and beliefs vibrate on a frequency scale.

Take a moment to think about a goal you want. What energy level is it vibrating at? Excitement? Anticipation? Then look at your beliefs, what's their vibration? Do the levels match? If not how can you change this? What needs to happen to move you upwards, one step at a time?

Very occasionally I meet people who say things like, "Well I can't be 7ft tall, just because I imagine it" (actually you can, if you learn how to walk on stilts), or "I can't become a famous singer because I can't sing" (have you heard some of those famous artists when they are singing outside of a recording studio?).

But joking aside, I've never worked with anyone who brought goals they didn't think could be achieved. Most people I've worked with want simple everyday things that make their life and that of others better. Things like: earning more money to give themselves and their families more free time to enjoy together or to buy nice things; making a difference in the world via the work they do; having loving and caring relationships; giving back to others in their community or to charities; travelling and having fun with their friends or improving their health so they can live long and fulfilling lives.

> *"Your present circumstances don't determine where you can go, they merely determine where you are starting from."*
>
> – Nido Qubein

Goals start with a (16 second) dream. Dreaming breathes life into an idea. Creating positive energy around the dream makes it believable, writing it down or drawing it helps it become real. When it starts to feel real it's time to take action.

Occasionally I've had the pleasure and joy to work with clients who had dreams such as taking clean water to a village in India where there wasn't any, or working with abused adults to help them gain confidence and belief in themselves so they could move from a place of victim to one of empowerment, or another client whose goal was to help clean up the beaches and rivers around the world.

And these and other clients I've worked with on big picture goals were often told by those around them that they were dreamers, unrealistic, their goals were impossible, one person couldn't make that much difference – but they did! Some of these clients thanked me for listening to them without judgment, for believing in them even when they weren't sure if they believed in themselves as it gave them hope; sometimes all it takes is one person who believes in you.

> *"A person who never made a mistake never tried anything new."*
>
> – Albert Einstein

Universal energy doesn't care how things have been in the past, it just cares about how things are now. It cares about what your starting point is **right now**, it cares about how you maintain your positive energy and flow on a day to day basis without attachment, desperation or need. Your current reality is a reflection of your current consciousness.

So it makes sense to choose how you use your mental and emotional energy wisely. Some people may worry unnecessarily, spend too much time worrying about what everyone else thinks, need to explain themself all the time, or pretend to be outwardly strong whilst feeling internally weak. Doing this will bring you more self-doubt, have you vibrating at a lower frequency and as you already know, cause you to attract more of what you don't want.

So the first step to help you change beliefs is look for and surround yourself with like-minded people who want to see you succeed. People who are there to support you even if you do fail.

- Who is it safe to show your vulnerability to?

- Who will be there for you without trying to rescue you?

- Who do you know who wants to help you succeed? Who do you know who sees things from your perspective or if they don't will challenge you from a place of love?

- Who might those people be?

By the way, I want to remind you that FAIL is a positive thing – it's your First Attempt In Learning – so like Thomas Edison, learn from every mistake and see it as an opportunity to try something different next time, that way you'll start to see progress however small it may be. But remember, it's important to do something new or different each time.

"Insanity is doing the same thing over and over again and expecting different results."

– Albert Einstein

Let's get you started. Think of a goal you want but you have some limiting beliefs about, write the goal down, next write down any limiting beliefs you have. Now take each limiting belief you have, one at a time, and write what you want instead. Make sure you write what you want, not what you don't want. This is important.

If like one of my clients you have a limiting belief that you aren't worthy of being loved or can never find a loving relationship, what might you want to believe instead?

Perhaps your new belief could be: "I love myself and I find it easy to attract a loving partner."

"There are two ways of spreading light, to be the candle or the mirror that reflects it."

– Edith Wharton

Many people find it difficult to actually say the words "I love myself " and mean them, so this might be a really good place to start working from, whatever your goal is, to help you vibrate at a higher level, because if you don't love (or at least like) yourself, what vibration are you sending out into the Universe? And how can you expect it to bring wonderful things to you if you don't believe you are worthy or loveable enough to receive them? It's worth thinking about.

On a scale of 1 – 10, how much do you like or love yourself?

Now you know what message you're reflecting out into the world.

Are you waiting for everything to be perfect before you start to love yourself? If so, did you know there is no perfect? Every day brings new challenges, to some of us more than others. Life is about challenge; everyone I've ever met has a really interesting story to tell. Some stories I've heard are really painful, really tough, but therapists tell us that challenge can be used to help build resilience and growth.

Maybe you'll get into an argument with someone, forget to keep your promise to eat healthily, skip going to the gym, someone will get the job you really wanted, you'll worry about things that later turn out to be unimportant, and for many of my clients (and I used to be the same), they end up beating themselves up verbally. Doing this will keep you on a low level frequency and it takes the higher levels to attract the good things you want into your life.

How can you start being nicer to yourself, kinder, more forgiving to yourself when things go wrong?

Doing this work will change your vibration, you'll begin to see nice things coming your way, but it does take a bit of practice. Please consider it.

Kay and Gay Hendricks, relationship counsellors who work with people to help them love themselves so they can find loving relationships say:

"Once you give yourself permission to love yourself exactly as you are, you set in motion a powerful effect. You free up all that energy you've been wasting in judging and rejecting yourself and you're able to channel that energy into finding creative solutions for those 'reasons' you thought you couldn't love yourself!"

Now that's got to positively affect your vibration one way or another.

Anyway, when it comes to writing what you want it's important to do just that, write what you want, which means leaving out the following words when you reframe your self-talk or write your positive statements:

- don't
- won't
- can't
- might
- try
- will

You can probably think of more, but I want to get the message across that when we write positive statements or affirmations, we need to state clearly what it is we want, and that means ignoring any negative language contained in the original limiting belief. It can take some practice but have a go (there are exercises to try on the downloadable playsheets), and if you find it difficult get someone to help you.

Make sure the new positive statements cover the four Ps:

- Personal
- Present tense
- Possible
- Positive

Then pick a date that sounds or feels realistic that you'd like it to be true by.

So let's look at that affirmation again:

'I' = **personal and present tense**

'love myself and I find it easy to attract a loving partner' = **positive**

Now, could this statement be **possible?**

If not, maybe consider using a bridge such as:

'Each day it gets a teeny bit easier for me to love myself because I…'

Fill in the gap, maybe you take a long bath, or go to the gym or say your affirmation in the mirror smiling at yourself as you do so.

Now repeat the new belief, hourly, daily, every time you see a red light, with a reminder on your phone, whatever it takes to help you remember, for practice makes for change, practice helps it become more permanent, practice changes your neurons, practice commits it to memory.

Make sure you have a go at this exercise even if it doesn't turn out to be the right one for you – after all, how can you know if you don't try?

> *"Not only does the world influence the mind*
> *but the mind influences the world."*
>
> – Gustav Fechner

Doing the above exercise will start to change your vibration, and as mentioned in the chapter Who You Are Physically, vibrationally speaking, like attracts like. Not only that, but you'll start to look for and see a different version of your previous world.

I read a great article by Dr Supriya McKenna titled *You find the person whose teeth fit your wounds.* Fab title that for me says it all, especially as there is a suggestion floating around 'out there' that you attract people, circumstances and situations into your life that fit the image you have of yourself. People and opportunities that match your vibrational frequency.

I've previously mentioned how your stories can trap you or how they can set you free, so I want to talk more about them in this chapter because of their importance. Be aware of the stories you tell yourself over and over again regarding why your life is the way it is. Such stories will keep you stuck in negativity and you won't be able to see what you do want when it presents itself let alone manifest it.

Unchallenged stories can chain you to your limitations, challenged ones can set you free. Your stories keep you in the loop. Your stories create your 'reality'. They're hypnotic, convincing, create the vibrations around your goals or desires and bring you more of what you say you do or don't want. Start to notice.

By recognising the stories you've been telling yourself and others, by becoming aware of them, by challenging them, you can start to change them, even if it's just a little bit at a time. In doing so, you can alter the influence they have on you, alter how you see the world and start to have the Universe bring you more of what you want instead of falling into the old trap, the old story, the old loop, which no longer serves you but is easy and filled with lower frequency vibrations. The choice is always yours.

"The past is never dead. It's not even past."

– William Faulkner

Candace Pert's work, referred to in chapter 2, is one of many that tell us that the state of your physical and mental health appears to alter the chemistry of your body and is impacted by your thoughts and beliefs.

If you're fed up with feeling frustrated, angry, sad or disappointed with an area of your life, it could be because you haven't taken time out to stop, notice and become aware of negative thinking, unchecked limiting beliefs, habits and unconscious drivers (which come from neural networks laid down because of past emotionally charged events) that are affecting your daily choices and behaviours.

Not only do these significant emotional events affect the emotional and psychological aspects of who you become, they also impact on your physical health. More and more work in the energy psychology field is providing evidence that the mind-body connection is not only real, but that healing can start when we challenge and change our negative thinking.

Even though many of your limiting thoughts may have come from your past or childhood, you don't have to have counselling to start to make positive change occur (though some may find it helpful), nor do you need to dwell on the past too long. What you do need to do is start to notice the things you think about yourself, other people and the world, are they positive or negative? Do they help you attract more or less of what you want? Are your thoughts really yours or were they a 'gift' from your caregivers?

It can be useful to write down limiting beliefs and negative thoughts as and when they come up (and if you wish, get clear about where they came from) so you can choose to keep them, call them out as falsehoods or change them.

From the reading I have done on neuroscience coaching to date, the suggestion is that it is important to write your negative thoughts and beliefs in a special book that is easy to find when you need it. This is important, because doing it this way calms the mind and frees up mental space which in turn may allow you to think of creative options that could help release old unhelpful or negative thoughts. If you write your beliefs on a sheet of paper you might lose it, so the mind will worry about that and use up important brain energy.

"Every change in the human physiological state is accompanied by an appropriate change in the mental-emotional state, conscious or unconscious, and conversely every change in the human mental-emotional state, conscious or unconscious, is accompanied by an appropriate change in the physiological state."

– Elmer and Alyce Green

We can intuitively tell the difference between good and bad information that we hear about or come across in our day to day lives. John Diamond wrote a book called *Our Body Doesn't Lie* about muscle testing. Behavioural kinesiology is where muscles are tested and respond to good or bad objects, emotions or people.

I learned muscle testing as part of my Thought Field Therapy training and have personally found it really useful in changing limiting beliefs as well as using it in my coaching career.

We all have what's known as a blind spot. The blind spot can unintentionally help you to ignore how you really operate or fib to yourself about how positive you really are. Muscle testing helps to communicate effectively with your subconscious mind and find beliefs you may be unaware of.

By becoming aware of how I was sabotaging myself I was able to handle the limiting beliefs from a place of honesty and respect, start to change them into positive beliefs and start to move towards what I wanted rather than what I didn't.

Muscle testing helps to communicate effectively with your subconscious mind, it can help you identify unconscious blocks in the form of negative or limiting beliefs. By becoming aware of any, you now have the choice to keep doing what you've always done or the opportunity to try something different. If you choose to do something different you can start to raise your energy vibration.

> *"Unless you make the unconscious conscious it will direct your life and you will call it fate."*
>
> – Carl Jung

Beliefs start as a thought, a thought that you think over and over again based on an experience, something you saw or something someone told you about yourself. As the saying goes, 'what the thinker thinks the prover proves'. It's nothing more than a story and it wasn't true until you made it so. Every word, every story vibrates at a frequency which will attract like-minded listeners, events or situations into your life.

Start paying attention to what you're listening to, who you're listening to, how you're feeling and what you're saying and check if it vibrates and is in alignment with what you say you want. Is your conscious mind saying it wants something good, something positive, but you find yourself hanging out with misery or negativity on a regular basis?

When I was training in Neuro Linguistic Programming one of the presuppositions I learned was that people respond to their experience, not reality itself, and in doing so start to look at the world through the filters of a belief system which make the beliefs held become real. In other words, we look to find that which we believe to be true.

Earlier in this chapter I mentioned that the conscious mind pays attention to around 7-9 things at any one time, whereas the 'subconscious' mind is there to make quick decisions and calculations based on your biases, values, beliefs and past experiences from the thousands of pieces of information it's bombarded with every second. Consciously you're only aware of a tiny fraction of them, because if you weren't, you'd have to deal with billions of unnecessary bits of information, which could give you a headache! So the excess is filtered by your sub/unconscious and it's an effective way for your brain to bring to your attention the things that are important, dangerous or need your immediate attention.

Often your subconscious and conscious minds aren't working together as one around a goal you desire, which means not vibrating at the same frequency as each other; this is known as parts separation. You know this is true if you're struggling to achieve the goal, have negative feelings about it or keep getting stuck at the same point. When this happens, there's a good chance your parts are out of alignment with each other and are in a tug of war. The subconscious usually wins.

Start to pay attention to what's going on; here are two useful questions to ask yourself:

"Is my behaviour compatible with what I desire?"

If not, what needs to be changed?

"Does my subconscious support my heart's desire?"

If you're not achieving your outcome then the answer may be no, so ask yourself if this is a 'should' goal, or if not, what you are fearful of. Then take action on the answer.

> **"Sometimes I've believed as many as six impossible things before breakfast."**
>
> – Lewis Carroll

Here's a goal of mine I decided to play with when I first understood the Law of Attraction. I remember saying to my now ex-husband that I wanted to see if this Law of Attraction really worked and he was fascinated to see too. We agreed we wouldn't tell anyone else, it was our light-hearted game around getting the car of 'my dreams'.

We'd never had a surplus of money, we had both always worked hard throughout our lives and I was careful with the small amount of money we had as paying the bills and looking after our children was my first priority.

Since my first Saturday job aged 12, I'd always saved something, my mother insisted I did and I was an obedient daughter. It was great she did as it allowed me to buy my first (of many) second-hand car when I was 18. It was a Hillman Avenger, lime green; I loved it. I'd saved for six years and to now be able to buy a car was so exciting.

As time went by, I was never fussed about what car I had, I just wanted it to run and get me from A to B. I remember not having a car when I was about 20 years old and my dad giving me his old Mini (that he'd painted with gloss white paint so it would stop rusting!) and me just being happy to have a car again. I remember a man at a petrol station saying to me, "What's a nice girl like you doing in an old banger like that?" I hope you get the point I'm making.

So the reason I'm telling you this is in 2006/7 I said to my husband that I really wanted a Mercedes Benz 230 convertible in silver! It didn't have to be new (I don't like the way they depreciate as soon as they're off the drive), but I wanted to see if it was possible to manifest it. We couldn't afford it. Historically I never bought anything I/we couldn't afford. At the time, I'd never paid more than £2,000 for a car.

Please remember, this is an odd goal for me, but I'd seen this car, loved how it looked and really didn't mind if I got it or not. But weirdly I expected I would. I cannot explain that, it was just a knowing, an absolute belief. But now you know about the universal laws, and I didn't at the time, you'll appreciate how they can work.

So, we both started to look out for them on the road, and were surprised how many there were, I'd never noticed them before this game (that's the RAS at work).

We saw there was one for sale at the local garage; excitedly, we booked a test drive, still no money. We started to talk about buying it, talk about it as though we had it (a lovely game), visualised getting into it and going places and laughing about it (the 16 seconds leading to 15 minutes a day exercise). Still no money. I was building my coaching business at this time and investing my time and whatever money I earned into it.

And then I had a knowing, an intuition that I would allow the work to come to me to buy it. And with that I bought the one we had test driven using a credit card for half of it and a debit card for the rest of it, all at six months' interest-free credit. Please know I'm not encouraging you to follow my unheard of and unusual method. I just knew the money was coming (and if it hadn't I'd have sold the car).

Of course you already know what happened. I bought it, we drove it with pleasure and joy, I carried on working the way I always had and the money started to come in, and by the time six months was up, I'd earned the extra money to pay off the car in full! We couldn't believe it. How could that be?

Though it was pretty and I enjoyed driving it, it wasn't my 'type' of car (when I studied sociology, I remember my teacher saying things like cars represented personalities, I didn't agree with him back then, but maybe he was right), so after a year I sold it and bought a different second-hand brand that is my 'type' and I've stayed with it to date. No, not gloss white painted Minis.

I've since done exactly the same thing in other areas of my life and I now know my pattern. It's not needing the goal to happen or working harder than normal, it's knowing what I want without attachment, knowing that it's coming with a real sense of trust and each time I've played the game, it's worked. Each time the energy behind the goal has been one of lightness, fun, non-attachment and expectation. There's never been any negative feeling or anxiety present, and you may recall these two used to be my best mates. I'm not sure it's something I can teach, it's just something I know. Something I *allowed* to happen along with taking inspired action – that's important.

If you can, it's worth thinking about events in your life where goals just happened and noticing what emotions were going on at the time. What was missing? (Normally fear.) What was present for you?

"We are what we repeatedly do."

– Aristotle

If you have any 'not good enough' or 'not worthy' or 'don't deserve' beliefs, it may be time to start looking for what you want from within. This can be done by working on accepting and loving yourself just the way you are, warts and all. It's an exceptional exercise, because when you accept you're OK the way you are (with the intention of being an even better version through personal development work), you raise your vibration.

"Everything we do is simple in the end, even though there's lots of complicated stuff."

– Professor Nate Lewis

Different authors suggest that we are most likely to be 'hypnotised' about the way the world is, who we are and what we believe from the ages of three to eight when we are operating in the theta and alpha brainwave states. Our brainwaves change depending on what we are doing and how we are feeling, they can be thought of as musical notes in terms of low, deep frequency waves up to high-pitched frequency waves. They are complex in terms of functioning and there are four states: Delta, Theta, Alpha, Beta.

I bring them to your attention because if the scientists and psychologists are correct, who we become as adults is programmed at a very early stage of our life when we are operating in Theta brain wave state, by adults who are operating from Beta state. Theta for adults can be found in hypnosis and many individuals find it useful to change old unhelpful beliefs formed in childhood by creating self-hypnosis recordings, seeing a hypnotherapist or purchasing readymade recordings for use at home.

"The greatest good you can do for another is not just to share your riches, but to reveal to him (her) their own."

– Benjamin Disraeli

The Law of Attraction is always working for you; you can check this by taking a mental look at your life right now. Do a sweeping visualisation of it, or draw a wheel of life[6] and see how happy or satisfied you currently are with your life. If you're honest with your scoring, it will show you a reflection of your beliefs and stories, the orders you've placed with the Universe and what you believe you're allowed to have. Even if you have done a wheel of life before or recently, try it with this new way of thinking.

"People have a hard time letting go of their suffering, out of fear of the unknown. Many people turn their backs on what it is that they really want in life, they prefer suffering that is familiar."

– Thic Nhat Hanh

In order to change limiting beliefs, you first need to recognise them. A limiting belief will be something that stops you from

---

6   A wheel of life is a bird's eye view of your life today; draw a circle, cut it into eight pieces, put your important areas of life into each segment, ie career, health, relationships, family, money, health, friends, community, personal development etc, then score them on a scale of 1-10 in terms of how satisfied you are with each area.

moving towards your goal or achieving your outcome. It could appear as a thought, as mind chatter, as a story that you weave into something huge which causes drama and pain (known as catastrophic thinking in Transactional Analysis, a really interesting psychological theory), as a negative feeling or images of doom and gloom. So before taking action on your goals, it could be useful to identify anything that might stop you from achieving them (see exercise 1 for this chapter in the downloadable sheets).

Limiting beliefs are just gaps that need identifying and filling. To do this, you need to become aware of them, then ask yourself, "What do I want to believe instead? I've got X, what do I want instead? What skills do I have (or need) that could help me? What experience do I need to change this belief? What do I need to develop within my character to allow me to move on from it?"

When I wanted to become a speaker and trainer I had to overcome many limiting beliefs and I'm so happy I did. As you know, I worked as an adult teacher which included personal development techniques, so when I trained as a coach, I loved the positive messages I got to share with my small classes so much, I wanted to share them with larger groups.

Though my teacher training had given me really useful skills regarding delivering information, the thought of standing in front of 100+ people frightened me. Maybe you've heard it's one of people's biggest fears. But I really wanted to share this new positive information, so if I was going to be successful I'd have to face my fears and take a look at my limiting beliefs which included things like:

- I don't know enough about the subject

- People might not be interested in what I have to say

- I haven't got a good enough memory, I'll forget what I need to say

- I don't know how to manage big groups

- I'm scared of being heckled

- If the technology fails I won't know what to do

- I'm worried I'll blush or mumble if I'm challenged

- What if I can't answer a question? I'll look foolish

- I'm going to shake at the beginning and lose control, my voice will go

There were more, but I want to give you an idea of the type of things that were going through my mind.

So I looked at my list (it was longer than above), and I started to sort them into different categories.

- **Weaknesses** – I'm scared of being heckled

- If the technology fails I won't know what to do

- I'm worried I'll blush or mumble if I'm challenged

- What if I can't answer a question? I'll look foolish

- I'm going to shake at the beginning and lose control, my voice will go

- **Areas for development** – I don't know enough about the subject

- People might not be interested in what I have to say

- I'll forget what I need to say

- I don't know how to manage big groups

- **Limiting beliefs** – I haven't got a good enough memory
- I'll forget what I need to say
- I'll blush or mumble if I'm challenged
- I'm going to shake at the beginning and lose control, my voice will go
- What if I can't answer a question? I'll look foolish
- **Facts** – I don't know how to manage big groups
- If the technology fails I won't know what to do

As you can see, I had a few weaknesses, areas for development, limiting beliefs and some facts. Next I needed to look at my strengths and skills.

- **Skills** – I know how to prepare a lesson; a presentation requires the same preparation
- I've been trained in how to deliver information in small pieces to help a group stay engaged
- I've been taught about different learning styles
- **Strengths** – I've been well trained, I've been regularly assessed with good feedback, I became a teacher trainer and assessor, I'm vigilant after a session at reflecting on what went well and what could be improved upon
- I'm good at planning and preparing
- **Facts** – I know the audience are coming because they are interested in my subject
- I know my subject well

So what do I need to **develop**? Belief, courage, managing my anxiety, deep breathing.

What do I need to **do**? Make a list of everything that could go wrong and then in a separate column write how I'll handle it if it does.

Know it's OK to say "I don't know the answer" to a question and offer it out to the audience, or say "I don't know that, let me find out before the event is over."

Think of a role model and 'step into her' visually, every day for two weeks, three times a day prior to my first big presentation so I can pretend I am her and act as she would and then anchor the good feelings (this is the fake it idea we've talked about).

I chose to start by writing down everything that could go wrong and how I'd handle it if it did. Thank goodness I did because many things went wrong! I handled them with just a little bit of panic:

- Projector and slides didn't connect
- I was told I was being assessed just as I went out to speak!
- I panicked, I forgot everything I wanted to say
- I started to shake
- I started delivering the middle of my presentation at the beginning

> *"Life can only be understood backwards;*
> *but it must be lived forwards."*
>
> – Søren Kierkegaard

Because I had rehearsed stepping into my role model and pretending to be her, as the panic hit, I stopped, took a deep breath (this simple thing can **never** be underestimated in terms of positive state change), asked myself what I said I'd do if these things went wrong, pressed my anchor, became my role model, smiled, said, "So what I wanted to start with is…" and everything flowed from there on.

I also made sure I was in the room early so I could see the audience trickling into the room and say hello to each one of them rather than walking into a room full of 100 people. I'd prepared and practised a 'script' which I'd learned by heart, I'd included exercises for the delegates to do so I didn't have to talk for too long at any time. I had slides to remind me of the next topic.

I got through it. I'd been so nervous my husband had driven me to the venue. When I came out, I was walking on air, he asked me how it went. "Great," I said, and "I'm never doing it again!" But of course I did and the rest is history.

The preparation I'd put in place equalled inspired action, it gave me clarity, focus and positive intention. Though my initial underlying vibration had been fear, by stepping into courage I started to flow. My intention was bigger than my fear; to share positive information with large groups of people, this met my value of purpose in my work which made me feel amazing. I continue to train large numbers of people to this day and I love it.

However, I think it's important to share that at the beginning of every training event I'm involved with, I still get butterflies and feel nervous before I start. I've reframed the butterflies as positive, they mean I'm still excited to deliver information to new audiences, in fact I say, "If they stop, I'll stop training."

The reason I share this story with you is because I found my strategy, one that works for me based on how I like to operate. I practised it and over time, with some tweaks, I grew confident. Some of my colleagues, family and friends said, "Just do it, jump in the deep end, it'll all work out OK." But in my world, with my reality that's not true for me. If I did it their way, I'd have fallen apart that day, I'd have let myself and others down, I'd have been upset. Are you noticing my 'story' here? I can afford to tell it to you and myself because it works in a positive way for me. If it didn't I'd need to change it. I share it because, regardless of all the good intentions and advice others gave me, I'm not them and it suits me to work the way I do to resolve a problem. It's taken me a lot of time to trust myself with this, but I'm glad I did because it feels good and it vibrates positively and it brings me more of what I want because of it.

What works for you? What's your style when it comes to solving problems or creating new exciting opportunities? Get to know and use it because the vibration will send out a signal to the Universe that you're ready to receive that which you want.

> *"Write it on your heart that every day is the best day in the year."*
> – Ralph Waldo Emerson

When you wake up in the morning what's the first thing you think or do? Do you stretch, yawn, smile and greet the day with joy? Or do you groan and feel sad you have to get up? Start noticing from tomorrow, because how you start your day as soon as you open your eyes (or even before) sets your vibration for the day. It's important you focus your thoughts and feelings on the energy you want to send out to the Universe right from the moment of waking. Doing this means that even when events happen that are outside of your control, you know you can handle them.

In *The 7 Habits of Highly Effective People* Stephen Covey writes about response versus reaction. Bad things can and do occur on a day to day basis, it's how you **choose** to respond to them that determines the vibration you send out and what you get back.

So from tonight, start thinking about how you'd like tomorrow to be for you and then, when you are ready, take a look at your downloadable playsheet 11.

Here's a final 'thought' based on Joe Dispenza's work, *The Tao of Quantum Physics.* Joe Dispenza is a thought leader, a motivational speaker, author and Law of Attraction teacher for some years.

He says: thoughts mixed with feelings create attitudes, a series of attitudes create beliefs, beliefs are constructed by our attitudes which are driven by our emotions which fuel our beliefs, chunk beliefs together and we have perception, all of which is determined by how we think!

He advises catching and changing any negative beliefs and replacing them with new ones because when we change our mind, we construct a new set of thoughts, and if we practise thinking these new thoughts over and over, we create a new neural pathway which allows our brain to recognise the new thought/belief as true.

Remember, if you really are ready to change your beliefs you will need to do something different; I know you know this but it's worth repeating. It will change your vibration. And if it helps, think of anything you have successfully changed or learned in the past, recall how that thing once seemed difficult or impossible but with time and practice it became possible and eventually easy, even a habit.

In order to grow, you have to move out of your comfort zone. It's important to stop doing what doesn't work and try new things that might (without attachment), just to see if they work or not. It's important to enter into the challenge as if it were a game and make it fun. It may feel a little uncomfortable at first but you can't grow unless you're willing to play a bit with what you don't know, and if you don't try you'll never know.

MYTH DEBUNK: Reading lots of personal development books is enough to manifest my goals.

MANIFESTATION METHOD: Pick one or two tips that feel good from the book, daydream about them for 16 seconds daily then take regular action before reading another book.

MYTH DEBUNK: There is a set of rules I have to follow in order to manifest what I want in my life or it won't work. I must be doing it wrong.

MANIFESTATION METHOD: Pay attention to your preferred learning style, what makes you feel good? Operate from there, your current consciousness creates your current reality.

To support you with this chapter please download and work with the playsheets: www.playsheets.16seconds.co.uk

In the next chapter you'll be introduced to creating your reality, the things that can get in the way of attracting what you desire and how to become aware and take inspired action.

CHAPTER 7

Creating Your Reality And The Benefit Of Inspired Goal Setting

Sandra

Reality. A scary word for some, maybe for most people depending on how their lives are working out for them. If life is going well then reality is a great thing and if not, then reality is something that we would prefer to shy away from if we possibly could, if life wasn't so apparent, so *real*. But regardless of whether our world is going well or not, we crucially either forget, or refuse to believe, or just don't realise that **we** create **our** own reality every second of every day.

Before you protest that there is no way you would create the reality that you're presently living, let me just explain how the creation of reality works and how you have unwittingly and unconsciously been preparing what you are currently living and how you can come to understand that you can shift your thoughts and vibration to consciously start creating the reality that you do want, instead of unconsciously creating the life you don't want. Truly, you can.

As I touched on in the chapter Who We Really Are Vibrationally (and I'm delving deeper about creating through thoughts, emotions and vibration in this chapter), everything is energy. And whether you believe it's the Law of Attraction that's picking up on what you think and feel, or whether your brain is taking you down the same familiar neural pathways of thoughts and behaviours (and it's usually both as everything is interlinked), nothing is created unless you think and feel it first.

Living a life of mediocrity?

If we truly believed this, we would logically do all we could to create our reality on purpose. Some do. But if it were as easy as that for busy, stressed, time-limited humans, we would be creating the life we want with ease and speed. But it's not like that, is it? Most are creating their lives by default, hoping that they can get to the end of their day successfully and hopefully with not too many mishaps. Many people in this faster than ever before world believe they don't have the time it takes to be aware of what they're thinking and feeling and shift it if it doesn't feel good. Time is of the essence, things need to be done, work needs to be prioritised, family needs to be prioritised and now thoughts and feelings too? It's all just too much!

So, the pay-off for this swirling around trying to get everything done is to be negligent with our creative focus. At any particular moment in time, if you're feeling good and thinking good thoughts then you are a vibrational match to creating a good experience. But the same is true the other way around and then you create a not so good experience. You are exercising no control over what it is you are creating and you live your life in response to the conditions around you, always hoping that things will work out OK. And hopefully, most of the time they do work out OK. But why just OK when you can create a reality that is what you truly want? A life that is fulfilling, prosperous, abundant, on purpose, fun-filled, vibrantly healthy, full of love and not to mention, happy! Why would you choose to create by default and live a life of mediocrity in comparison to what you could consciously and deliberately create?

So, if we believe that we can create our reality (and if you're reading this book I am going to either assume you do believe we can create our own reality and want to know more or you are at least curious about the concept), why do we not take the time to prepare ourselves to create what we want?

1. **Laziness**. Recent scientific research has shown that the amount of effort required to do something influences what we think we see. The study which was performed under an international collaboration between UCL (London), NICT (Japan) and Western University (Canada) came to this conclusion after conducting a series of experiments that tested the willingness of participants to choose the harder of two tasks. The setup was simple: A cloud of dots on a computer screen moved either left or right, and the person playing the game used the levers at their left or right sides to signal which direction the dots were moving in. When

the scientists surreptitiously started adding weights to the levers, the participants began to see things differently. If the dots were moving left, but the left-hand lever was harder to pull, they tended to see the dots as moving to the right — which was the easier choice. The same thing happened when the weight was put on the opposite side. In other words, the participants unconsciously shifted their view of reality just so they wouldn't have to work harder than they had to. As lead author Nobuhiro Hagura PhD concluded: "Our brain tricks us into believing the low-hanging fruit really is the ripest. We found that not only does the cost to act influence people's behaviour, but it even changes what we think we see."

So what we see is influenced by what we feel. When we make decisions to act (or not), the brain thinks like an economist and runs a cost-benefit analysis. If the 'cost to act', as the researchers call it, is too high, it can bias our decision-making process, making us less likely to do things. So when you usually enjoy going to the gym and we enter into the winter months and darker nights, it is much harder for people to continue their routine because they are influenced by what they see, ie the darker nights, and begin to feel it would be easier to remain indoors as the evening 'draws in' even if it's not that cold outside, because it appears to be the easier option! We're psychologically prepared to live the easiest life, even if it's not a life we want. If it's easy and it 'makes do' then that's enough. Welcome to mediocrity!

But as we are primed for ease, we can make it so much easier to achieve the life we truly do want if we believe we can create it by our vibrational thoughts and emotions. As the research has shown, we as humans don't like going down the hard route, so choose the easy route. How difficult is it to take an initial 16 seconds to imagine what you would like to be, do or have and then build on that time as you have fun with the process? Really enjoying creating your life. Visualising, imaging, creating, having fun – does that sound like hard work? No. But it feels hard when you're not getting instant results by doing this process, and then once again, those pesky neural pathways in the brain will lead you back to the same old familiar patterns of behaviour. This feels easier because, once again, the belief that you've held most of your life that you can't create your own reality becomes uppermost once more, and although this doesn't necessarily feel good, it feels comfortable. And then change feels hard and you exchange the possibility of living an extraordinary life with living a life of mediocrity.

2. **Instant gratification**. Most people are looking for instant gratification. In this busy, fast world we live in, we want what we want and we want it now. No waiting. Now. So we will go for whatever feels quick and easy, even if it means compromising what we really want and what we could create and instead we end up settling for a lesser version.

I have seen this so many times in my work supporting thousands of people to lose weight. They have a vision of what they want to create and they really do want it. They are completely fed up with how they perceive themselves and what they look and feel like and they are ready to do something different to make the change needed to bring about this 'new version' of themselves. But because they don't see the weight loss coming off quick enough, which then means it becomes a real effort, they become disheartened. They don't believe they can follow through. It becomes 'hard work' and they go back to their old habitual pattern of behaviour with food and exercise because it's easier and they settle for feeling mediocre about their body, instead of feeling at peace and appreciative of what they could have achieved.

The irony of it all is that if you keep heading towards what you want, continually reinforcing the new pattern of thought and behaviour, it then becomes a habit and your new way of being becomes easy! But wanting instant gratification gets in the way of allowing your new attitude to become the new norm and thereby sabotages what you really want. You could make it so much easier by taking 16 seconds and align with the new vision, feel good about it, feel the emotions of how it will be when you cross the finish line and have fun with the idea of creating what you want. And if you were really feeling the fun, your neural pathways wouldn't be trying to find the easy route as having fun feels and is easy!

3. **Shoulds.** How can we begin to create a life we want when we feel we 'should' be doing something else? Despite wanting a different job, relationship, more money, a healthier body, our actions show that we shouldn't be creating the life of our dreams, we 'should' instead be living and dealing with the life we have already created by the thoughts, beliefs and vibration that we are presently living. We 'shouldn't' be having fun, we 'should' be fire-fighting and making sure everyone else is OK. But in the meantime, the life you want to live is not having the attention it needs to flourish into the reality that could be yours, if you allowed yourself to attend to it. Is it truly so difficult to build on 16 seconds to

have fun creating, visualising, feeling into the life you do want? Are you going to allow your brain to take you back to your habitual thoughts of 'I should be doing something else with my visualising time – what about the children and their needs? What about my partner? What about work?' This just reinforces the old picture that you've been living.

But it can be easy, if you allow it to be. You need to decide, are you worth the daily investment of initially 16 seconds to create, to have fun, to allow the life you do want. Do you really have the time to not create the life you want, because you are too busy ensuring that you are doing and living a life that feels right and comfortable for others? Welcome to the No.1 regret of the dying – living life to others' expectations instead of your own. Is that the reality you choose to create?

4. **Procrastination.** This old chestnut! Procrastination can trip you up – it can fool you into believing you are taking action to create the life you want. If you take the tiniest step towards a life that resembles the life you would eventually like to be living, you could congratulate yourself on this action and believe that's enough (for now). You don't know when you'll do more, but you've done something. You can now give yourself unconscious permission to do other things that have absolutely no bearing on what you do want. You make excuses and as Brian Tracey (motivational speaker and self-development author) said, you end up living on 'Someday Isle' – 'Someday, I'll do this…', 'Someday, I'll create the life I want.' As I've explained when writing about laziness, it's easier to remain in a life that you are living. But life moves very quickly and you could end up being at the end of your life still procrastinating, still delaying, but there

is now no place to go, no more time left to continue stalling. We didn't take the chance to create a magnificent life for ourselves. We allowed comfort and fear to take over. Which leads us to…

5. **Fear.** It really doesn't matter if it's fear of failure, fear of success, fear of others' judgments or opinions – it is still a hurdle to creating the life that feels right for you. It is a feeling that keeps you frozen, keeps you stuck. It doesn't matter at all if the fear-based thought is rational or not – you feel it. You panic and the amygdala in the brain kicks in, sending you a shot of cortisol and adrenaline, puts you in the fight or flight response and any hope you had of creating the life you want is shut down. And that is what tends to happen to most people – you have a desire and you shoot it down within roughly one to two seconds as your brain tells you of the difficulty, the impossibility of getting what you want, the differing opinions of others, the stupidity of the idea and you then close down to the desire that you, just a few short seconds ago, thought was so exciting.

Intention, clarity and focus – your best friends

So, we know what stops us creating our reality, but what can help us with the creation process? How do we actually know what we want? How can we have clarity over *our* desires when there are so many outside influences – parents, friends, partners, peers and now the ever consistent social media? How can you know uniquely and clearly what *you* want?

The first thing is to acknowledge is that it's OK to have an experience that clarifies what you don't want so that you have complete clarity over what you *do* want. We are so keen to keep the status quo because then everything remains stable and there is no rocking the boat that we don't allow our daunting experiences the significance to bring about clarity and to effect change. But these clarifying moments are the first step to creating what it is you do want: to create your new reality. We all want something, whether it's more money, good health, love, we are all usually in the state of desire, but we only create our reality if we have a clear desire without any dilution of its strength. The clarity of desire leads to clarity of thought, which then leads to clarity of action, the first step to creating the reality you **do** want.

So, alongside clarity, what is the importance of focus? Once you have clarity, focus is everything. How can we attract what it is we do want if we don't remain focused on the desire? Imagination is the first step to creation. Imagination is focus. Imagination focuses on the desire that you want.

If you search for the meaning of 'imagination', one of the Google responses is as follows: "**Imagination** is the **process** by which the mind creates images, possible outcomes, and other thoughts that have not been directly observed or experienced in reality." You cannot imagine without focus. Even if you imagine by daydreaming about what it is you want or how it would feel if you had it or what it would look like, you are still focusing – your desire is still your point of focus regardless of the process you are using to create that desire.

We are here as creators. We are here to create the present and therefore the future, as we want it, but is that your intention? Intention, clarity and focus all go hand in hand to create the most wonderful life that is yours to have purely because you want it. It is imperative you have the intention to be clear, to focus, to believe that what you want is all ready and waiting for you, just waiting for you to become a vibrational match to your desire. Lined up for you to feel what it feels like to have what you want – the feel good feeling, the appreciation, the knowing that having it is a 'done deal' and from this inspired place, taking inspired action.

It's now a pretty well-known story of how Jim Carrey, the actor, actually visualised, imagined and created the reality of his career and the abundance that came with it. Forgive me if you already know the story, but I think it is well worth repeating as it illustrates perfectly what I've just said. So Jim Carrey was an unknown Canadian actor, who arrived in Hollywood and would regularly daydream and imagine his life as a successful actor, working with directors and writers he respected. He would also drive every evening and park outside these respected Hollywood professionals' homes in Mulholland Drive and just imagine what it would be like to be living there as a movie actor. Not only did he continue with this practice, he also wrote himself a cheque for $10m for 'acting services rendered' and dated it Thanksgiving 1995. Three years later, just before Thanksgiving 1995, he received $10m for the movie *Dumb and Dumber*.

The key to this wonderful creation was his clear intention, his clear desire and the *consistent* focus he had while visualising what he wanted. He also **believed** it. He believed he already had his desired, hugely successful career and it *felt* good. It wasn't in his physical reality right at that point and that was OK because he felt good by imagining and visualising the very thing that he wanted. It felt better to Jim to create his reality and, as a result, to feel all the wonderful feelings that came with that vision than to focus on his current (temporary) reality.

Should actions and goal setting

Firstly, can I just say that if you don't like the word *goal* and a lot of people don't, please substitute any word that feels better for you when you read the word goal in this book. Maybe aim, desired result, target etc – whatever feels good for you and matches your map of the world.

As a coach, it may come as a surprise and appear to be counterintuitive when I speak to my clients about not taking action towards any goal, unless it is *inspired* action towards an *inspired* goal. You may wonder what is the difference between an action and an inspired action, a goal and an inspired goal? The difference is all-important and is critical to you creating the life you want to create.

We've spoken briefly about should. Now let's speak about should in relation to goals. 'Should goals' are those that are normally dictated by other people or circumstances. Circumstances such as a mortgage, dependants, social conditioning, culture, comparison (usually negatively) of ourselves to others and a myriad of other dictates that surround us, and, without realising (and before reading this book), we set goals accordingly. Think of your own life – how many times have you decided to do something because it was driven by other people or circumstances? Think of the number of students that drop out of their university course because it isn't what they wanted to do, but allowed themselves to feel the pressured 'should' of their parents?

Again, in my role supporting thousands of people to lose weight, the large majority 'wanted' to succeed, not because *they* truly wanted to, but because parents, partners, family or their doctor wanted them to. But the thing about *should* is that it will never motivate a person to achieve their goal. It will motivate to a certain extent, such as getting that person to a weight-loss coach in the first place, but it won't succeed in keeping that person motivated through the shift in behaviour and eating patterns. To make such a shift and to change habits of a lifetime, the desire has to be strong and inspired. A clear intention of 'I'm doing this regardless...' The feeling that you *have to* do something will not inspire you to the finish line (in ordinary circumstances).

In my experience, the people who were told they should come to me to lose their excess weight didn't even complete the initial six sessions and they were clients who knew that losing weight would considerably help reduce their risk of a stroke or diabetes. And of those people who did achieve their weight-loss goal, less than 8% would keep their weight off for five years after getting to goal. Why? Because the personal desire isn't strong enough to keep up with the behaviour change that is needed to achieve that goal. If a goal has been put in place through a *should* suggestion, we either don't achieve it or we doggedly work towards it and any actions taken will be filled with resentment, inauthenticity (as it's not our goal), and lethargy.

We can also impose our own should, which again will backfire as it's not an inspired desire that's driving you, but some other need. Let me explain with a personal experience. I got engaged at the age of 19 because I wanted to go on holiday. To go on holiday was a desire but certainly not an inspired desire – more a 'everyone's doing it' desire. The engagement was a should. I wanted to go on holiday with my boyfriend of four years and another couple, but my boyfriend was from a culture where this wasn't acceptable unless we were engaged. Although my parents didn't want me to get engaged, unless I wanted it (and I truly didn't see the need), I did follow through with the engagement. I went on holiday, but looking back I could have said yes to the holiday and no to the engagement and forged my own way through, feeling into what felt right for me. But my main driver, my need, was not to upset anyone. I could upset *me*, but not anyone else. I wanted to keep the boat stable, not cause ripples and in the meantime, I took an action that felt compromising, inauthentic and a big *should*. A should that was imposed by me. And it then set a precedent for what was to follow.

Moving forward six years and now having lived with the same boyfriend for two years, we were told that within his culture, if we wanted to continue living together, we would have to do that as a married couple. Marriage *had to* be the next step. So again, feeling like that proverbial snowball rolling down the hill, gathering momentum, I said OK. Arrangements were made for a very big wedding (not *my* desire) and I returned to my parents' home the night before the wedding to sleep in my old bed. Except I couldn't sleep because I knew I was doing something that wasn't *my* dream.

The next morning, my mum turned to me without any other words being spoken about the wedding and said, "You don't have to do this." My mum was giving me an escape from my self-imposed should and what did I say? "I'm good Mum, it's all good." And why did I finally walk down the aisle truly hoping someone would rescue me? Because I knew how much money my mum and dad had to borrow to pay for a wedding that I didn't want, and as far as *I* was concerned, this was a definite 'should' moment that I must follow through on. My husband and I divorced a year later. My 'should' goal and subsequent actions definitely backfired on me and also on those around me who ironically I was trying to protect.

The vibrational impact of shoulds on the creation of your reality

So, let's go a bit deeper into understanding the impact of creating a reality that you don't really want has on you and your ability to create what you truly *do* want. When you operate from a 'should' thought vibration, you have then cut yourself off from all that you truly are. You have cut yourself off from your own power and you know this because of the way you feel. You don't feel good (even if you believe you're doing it for the good of others). You can feel compromised, resentful (over time), angry, sad and sometimes depressed and yet all of this was your own doing. Fundamentally, whenever you are going down a path that is in opposition to what feels authentically good to you, you blame others for the fact that you were the one who decided to do it!

Blame is easier to dole out than to accept responsibility for the decision you have made. And you are very likely unaware that you are doing it. Blame is such an ingrained habit from our younger years. How many times did you say, 'It wasn't me'? Or 'It's not fair'? By accepting that you and you alone are responsible for how you feel and what you do, you can then make an empowered choice to edge up the emotional vibrational scale and take action towards creating your reality from that delicious connection to all that you are and to that ever flowing stream of consciousness that is always there to guide and inspire you. When you operate from a place of should, you shut that flow off. When you allow your decisions to come from a place that feels emotionally right for you, you open the door to allow all that you desire to flow to you. The choice of which way to go – should or inspiration – is always up to you.

Inspired actions and goal setting

But what does it mean to take inspired action? And what is an inspired goal and how do you know if it is, indeed, inspired? It really is incredibly simple. The thought of the goal *feels good*. It feels *inspired*. The thought of the actions to achieve what it is you want *feels good*. It feels *inspired*. That truly is all there is to it. Anything that truly feels good is inspired. But, as I said earlier, you trample on that wonderful, inspired idea by bringing in old, redundant patterns of thought that tell you 'how difficult' it will be and you 'might as well give up now'. So you have *received* this amazing inspired thought leading you down the path to what you want and you have probably given it less than a second of air time before you have dismissed it through your belief of what you 'should' be doing instead. This is living someone else's life, not creating your own.

Let's recap on what is a *received* thought. It's an inspired thought that just pops into your head at a time when you weren't thinking of anything in particular. A headspace that was emptier than usual. As I mentioned earlier in the book, my received thoughts tend to come through when I'm cleaning my teeth! I'm just in an almost vacant space of enjoying the cleaning process and bang! A random thought pops in about work or life in general that I wouldn't have had the space or presence of mind to conjure up, and when it comes through, it's a thought that feels good – a mini 'aha' moment. That is a thought or goal to act on.

This hasn't come from the limited personality part of you. This has arrived through your connection to the ever flowing presence of energy vibration that has landed due to detaching from those noisy, seemingly ever present, busy thoughts for a few precious moments and it feels good. It feels inspired. If you allowed that thought to continue (instead of shutting it down), after 16 seconds the Law of Attraction would take hold of that inspired thought and bring you more thoughts like it. You would feel inspired to take action – to go to a place that you wouldn't have thought of, or to be 'nudged' to look up at a tube poster on your way to work, giving you the precise information that you're looking for. Or you will meet someone at a function who says something that resonates with you and it prompts you to take action.

There is no such thing as an accident in this Universe – just carefully coordinated rendezvous that are being orchestrated every moment of every day to help you create the life you want in the easiest, most flowing, joyful way, but only *if* you are open to acting on an inspired, good feeling thought instead of dismissing it as something random. This is the fun of creating a life that feels wonderful to you and resonates with who *you* are at your core. This is a life that is truly inspirational.

So, let me see if a personal example of when I took action on how I *felt,* instead of operating from a should can illustrate this for you on a practical level. Geographically in the world, a place I love and feel an affinity with is Bali. I have a real affection for its people, gentle culture, beauty and the loving energy of the island. When I'm there it supports my connection to all that I am and after our first visit to Bali, I remarked to my husband Martin that I would love to spend three months travelling around Bali. Martin, being action-oriented, went to his place of employment and arranged a three-month unpaid sabbatical that allowed him to spend that time in Bali.

Coming home after applying for and arranging the sabbatical, he very gleefully told me what he had done and that we could begin to arrange the trip for the following year! Instead of feeling excited anticipation of this long trip to a place I love, I just felt a big NO! The timing didn't feel right. It felt rushed. And although Martin had now cleared a significant hurdle for him in relation to going, I had only expressed a clear, inspired desire of travelling to Bali. I didn't know when, or how we would do it. I didn't want my limited brain to do the work by choosing forced action, I wanted to feel inspired and this felt far from inspiration. Although he had taken action from excitement and a practical need to put certain practices in place at work, I wasn't ready to move forwards towards it. The desire was clear, but the action to move towards it, wasn't.

Although I am blessed to be able to work from anywhere in the world (that has wifi), I hadn't spoken to my face to face clients about the possibility of our sessions being virtual for three months and I also have a regular (joyful) responsibility to a coaching organisation that I work alongside and being away for three months would impact quite severely on them. These weren't limiting thoughts I was having, these were emotions that I was experiencing which didn't feel good when I thought about the trip to Bali. And so I acted on the guidance system of my emotions and said to Martin that I wasn't ready to go and that I didn't know when I would be as three months away didn't feel good right now. Taking action and going to Bali from a feeling place of concern, worry and just a general 'this doesn't feel right' would come from a *should* place of following through on Martin's action of obtaining a sabbatical and not wanting to let him down. But by letting myself (and my emotional guidance system) down would have led to another spectacular backfire!

And so, despite his disappointment and not being able to answer his question of "When will you be ready?", I let go of thinking about the trip to Bali and trusted in remaining open to inspired thought and guidance whenever that would have a chance to flow through.

Trying to stay focused and feeling stressed with finding a solution to the Bali trip would have closed me down to my vibrational allowing of a much easier solution and to the expanded creating that the brain can also assist with when we are in a relaxed state.

So, I just went about my business, putting the trip to Bali to the back of my mind and instead just appreciating the life I was currently living and not thinking or worrying about a possible solution. One day, a couple of months after I said no to the three-month trip, I was walking down a road in a leafy part of London where I live, just appreciating the nature and feeling very good, not consciously thinking about anything at all other than the nature around me, and a random thought (a *received* thought) popped into my head out of the blue – *'You can go for 10 weeks!'* The change in duration wasn't even something I had thought about, but boy, did it feel good! Ten weeks instead of twelve immediately felt freeing. It felt great. I knew that the way my work was structured within the coaching organisation, this would work very well, even though it was only a difference of two weeks.

I also knew from this place of feeling good that working with my clients from the other side of the world would be a wonderful experience for both them and myself as I could time our trip over the summer when a few of them would be away for their own holidays for a portion of the time. They wouldn't lose the coaching support and it would be a fantastic acknowledgment that I could, indeed, work from anywhere, an amazing feeling for me as my top value is freedom. This then became an excited, inspired, absolute hell yes! Every time I thought of it, I felt great. My husband was thrilled. My clients were happy. It all worked well with the coaching organisation and the whole planning of the trip just flowed – even down to being guided to wonderful business class airline seats at a fraction of the usual cost! And we had the most joyful trip travelling through Bali and the Borneo jungle in Malaysia. So let's just recap on creating an easy flowing, desired life using this example of *inspired* goal setting and *inspired* action:

- The goal of going to Bali was inspired – it came from the heart, or for some, the gut and I didn't close down to the idea of going, by thinking or worrying of how or when or 'what if?'

- I felt and listened to my emotional response when Martin facilitated his unpaid sabbatical in order to go to Bali and *acted on my emotional guidance*, regardless of his disappointment.

- I stayed open to the idea of going, but I let go of the attachment to the outcome and instead just carried on with my practice of being in a general allowing state and appreciating on a daily basis, and thereby staying open to *receiving inspired thought*.

- I recognised the *inspired* thought popping into my head, felt the *good feeling thoughts and emotions* that resulted from it and took *inspired* action from the *inspired* thought. And as I did this, so I received more and more inspired thoughts that felt great concerning the trip as the Law of Attraction grabbed hold of this good feeling and brought to me more thoughts like it, such as guiding us to the cheaper business class airline seats, as an example.

The benefit of inspired action/goal setting?

I'm hoping that from sharing a couple of personal experiences with you, creating a life coming from inspired thought, instead of operating from a place of should, feels joyful, easy and flowing. But more important than anything, you are on this planet to feel good. Full stop. You are here to create a life that feels good to you. You are here to feel good when creating that life. This is about you. You aren't here to create a compromised life because of taking action from a place of duty or martyrdom.

This is about understanding that you have the best GPS system on the planet to create your desired reality – your emotions. They are guiding you every moment of every day on which path feels good (or not). Your mission – if you choose to accept it – is to trust that your emotional guidance system knows better than anyone or anything else in relation to you creating the best life possible for you. If it doesn't feel good, you listen to that quiet voice that says 'step away' and take action accordingly. And if it feels clear and there's that flutter of excitement in your heart or gut and that quiet voice which is saying 'hell, yes!' you act on that guidance, even if you don't know all the details right now. Trust that the details will fill in as you build the good-feeling momentum. This is how you mould and create the joyful expansive desires of your life. Have fun with the journey.

MYTH DEBUNK: As long as I have a goal, the Universe will deliver.

MANIFESTATION METHOD: You manifest what you want through your *emotion* connected to your thoughts. When you are thinking of your desire, be aware of how you *feel* about this desire. If this goal *feels* good to you, then build the thoughts you have around it and create it. If this goal feels uninspiring or a 'should', bring your thoughts away from it until you may, one day, feel excited about it. Create what you want by ideas and thoughts that *feel* good. Your emotions are your fuel to your thoughts, so use your fuel wisely.

Download the playsheets with short exercises to help you create and live your inspired life, full of potential and authenticity: www.playsheets.16seconds.co.uk

As we are coming to the end of the book, in our final chapter we are looking forward to supporting you with not only moving into the life you want, but also how to maintain the change that you have now begun to implement through the processes and tools within this book.

CHAPTER 8

Moving Forward And Maintaining The Change You've Started To Create

Sandra and Pam

So here we are, almost at the end of the book. How are you feeling? From the information you've received within this book and all the different techniques we've shared, you may have already made some incremental changes to the way you think, feel and believe about everything in your life that you want to alter or create.

The most powerful message we want to convey is that you *can* create your own reality by being aware of how you are currently stopping what you want, and therefore tweaking your perspective of thought in relation to what you want to be, do or have. By understanding the part the brain plays in preventing you stepping outside of your comfort zone **and** the strong force of the Law of Attraction (not to mention the other universal laws we have written about) and how it responds to your vibrational standpoint within 16 seconds, you now have the awareness and tools to allow the manifestation of your dreams. And we don't say that lightly. So, as you move forward into creating the life you desire, we want you to be consciously aware of and putting into practice the knowledge we've shared with you.

Stand out light bulb moments make a further fundamental difference to your vibrational standpoint and what you attract on a moment to moment basis. We are hoping you have found your light bulb moments within this book, and in this final chapter we would love to share with you what we have known, from our own experience, to have been pivotal learnings that have supported us in creating the life we truly love.

This book contains factual and researched knowledge on how to shift your individual perspective about the way you think and believe in relation to your life and we are hoping that by telling you of our own individual 'aha' moments from which we consciously live by and which we have touched on in earlier chapters in a more general way, may shed further light on what you need to know to create what you want and challenge any myths you previously believed.

Sandra

Care About How You Feel

This is absolutely number one for me. Caring about how I feel as a priority ensures I can maintain my vibrational connection to the universal energies and what it wants to provide for me. If I feel good, I am in a state of allowing and if I am allowing, then I am sending out a ripple of wonderful energies that not only are going to support me in attracting what I want, but will also support those around me and those I come into contact with. I truly believe I am on this planet as a teacher and an uplifter and I cannot follow through on my purpose if I am letting my emotional, physical, mental and spiritual wellbeing peak and trough depending on what's going on around me, and being swayed by other people's moods, perspectives and actions.

This though seems to be the number one difficulty for most people that I have worked with. The belief is that it is incredibly selfish for us as individuals to be aware of how we feel and then do whatever it takes to feel better. The general consensus is, if one of our friends or family is feeling down, then we should get down with them. Commiserate from the lower vibration in which they are standing. Why would you do that? Yes, it may feel comfortable for them to have you on their level, but how does that help them or you? You have to decide – are you here to feel good, and by standing true in that commitment not only allowing what you want to flow to you, but also supporting others to gently move up the emotional guidance scale? Or are you here to sway like a tree in the wind, blowing one way or the other depending on what's going on with the people or the world around you? You are then in resistance to all the abundance that is waiting for you. Waiting for you to decide to feel good, to open your arms and embrace the fun of life. It's a bit like climbing a greasy pole – you manage to scramble up, only to slip right back down again, just as you feel you may have a foothold. It becomes frustrating and exhausting.

About a year ago, my 25-year-old daughter (who has seen me live by these principles for as long as she can remember) came into my office as I was working and said, with hands on her hips, "Mum, is your vibration more important than me?" I answered, "Yes." She then asked, with an even stronger hands on hip stance, "Is it really?" I answered, "Yes." She then asked in an exasperated tone, "Even more important than your daughter?" And I answered once again, "Yes," but I also added that if I didn't focus on how I felt first and come from that centred place of unconditional ease, I would be unable to help her or others. My ripple effect would be more doom and gloom, not coming from objective upliftment. I think she finally understood it when I said, "And that's what I want for you too. I want your vibrational state to be more important than me, more important than anything." She then realised that was where her true power lay. I check in with how I feel throughout the day and if I can feel the beginning of a momentum of something that doesn't feel good, I will recognise it, not focus on the root or cause of it and look for any small thing to appreciate or feel good about, unconnected to the original condition.

Kindness to others has to also be offered to us. What virtue is there in believing that kindness stops at your door and never crosses your threshold? It is so interesting that when I work with clients and we discuss their values and kindness is stated as one of their driver values, they naturally find it extremely important to be kind to others, but they never think of being kind to themselves! So imagine, if kindness is one of your top values and you're not extending it to yourself, something will feel off. It won't feel congruent with who you are. It is not selfish to be kind to yourself first and then extend that kindness out in the world. It is a blessing that you can give from a clear place of authentic willingness and openness. It is not coming from 'if I give this, I might get that...' which is certainly not open and it comes from lack, not from the authentic you that is abundant and easy and in flow with the energies of the Universe.

When you feel good about yourself, you can appreciate yourself. You can feel empathy for your learning along the way. You can appreciate your body and what every blood vessel, cell, bone, nerve, muscle and organ does in supporting you in perfect wellbeing. You are able to pat yourself on the back for any small step you take towards a future that feels brighter for you. You can feel the peace of mind that ease brings. You notice the smiles that you may get as you're walking out and about because you know that as you feel good, so you are attracting evidence of it. The only vibrational arrows that are making their way to you are love, ease, connection, abundance and more things to appreciate. Wellbeing is the basis of all and a focus on feeling good cannot be understated. It is my daily focus and I can't think of a better way to start my day than creating a vibrational set-point of attracting more wellbeing.

Segment intending

This is an amazing process that I was taught by Abraham-Hicks and it is something once again I do on a daily basis. This is a perfect way to be the creator you are and create the day or the outcome you want. As we have said before, most people are reactors. There tends to be a situation that comes into your experience and you react. It really doesn't matter what emotion you are feeling that is causing you to react (fear, worry, anxiety), you react. But you cannot react and create what you want at the same time. You just can't – the Law of Polarity and the Law of Attraction will ensure that your *reaction* will bring you more conditions to match up with the fear, worry or anxiety that you are feeling, which is likely to be the polar opposite of the ease, peace of mind and abundance that you are looking for.

So, instead of just getting up in the morning and falling into your day, tired, rushing around trying to get ready for wherever it is you need to get to, and feeling more and more irritable and frustrated, you can choose to create the day ahead before you even get out of bed. Segment intending is when you literally intend how you want each part of your day to go, coming from clarity and enjoying the process of creating your day. Each segment of intention only takes a couple of minutes and sets the vibrational expectation of what's coming next within 16 seconds.

Let me give you an example of what I do. As I mentioned in the chapter Bridging the Gap, I intended an outcome when I travelled home on the Underground system, when apparently the trains weren't working efficiently in the direction of where I wanted to go and I received the outcome I intended, which was an easy and speedy journey home, all in flow and perfect timing. I consciously choose to intend each part of my day, not coming from a hope, a wish or struggle but with real knowing that I create my day by the vibrational intention I set and then I allow the laws of the Universe to do their magic. This is acknowledging how I want each part of my day to be, whether I focus by writing it down or just take a couple of quiet moments to focus on what I want. I then clearly intend the outcome and follow through with inspired action.

So, let me be more specific about how I intend my day. When I wake up, before I get out of bed and start my day I focus on the ease and flow of my morning, having fun with my morning process and feeling into the appreciation of my coffee, my nutritious breakfast and getting ready effortlessly for my first client. I then intend a wonderful session for my client and myself prior to each session. If I have a meeting lined up that day, I will intend the outcome I want depending on the subject, but I will always intend ease, flow and fun. At the end of my working day, I will intend the most wonderful dinner and a loving and joyful evening with my husband, family or friends. And when I'm getting ready for bed, I will intend a deep, soothing sleep leading to waking up in the morning fully refreshed.

Intending these different segments of my day only takes a couple of minutes of being quiet, having clarity over what I want and being clear with my intention. The vibration of my intention then ripples out, allowing the lining up of the universal energies to attract the very thing I want. Not only does this work so well, but I feel so good creating the day I want. It's fun, easy and the results are amazing. Please practise this. You will soon see your day working out as you truly intend it to be. If you don't have real clarity with what you want in your day and your feelings and the words you are saying aren't a match (you aren't feeling the positivity that your words may be expressing), you will also see the struggle of your day. But either way, the outcome is wonderful proof that you create your reality.

Go general

This was so helpful for me when I learned about this many years ago. The 'go general' rule helps to create something you want, where the specifics of that particular thing is causing you to wobble. This wobble usually stems from wanting your desire so much and you're worrying about not getting it (lack vibration). Or the specifics of what you want feels quite unbelievable in ever achieving it and therefore is leading to worry, anxiety and panic.

I clearly remember a time when I was about to deliver my first leadership training and I was extremely nervous. I was trying to intend how I wanted the day to turn out – successful teaching where the delegates could understand, participate and learn everything that they wanted in a fun, easy way. But when I was thinking of the specific training, the content of the training, the specific delegates, it was enough to throw me into a tail spin and I was completely in a wobble and unable to intend any outcome at all! So, I remembered – go general! By not thinking about any specific details, the pressure lifted immediately.

I thought about what the very end of the day would look like; I thought about the dinner I would have with my husband and how I would be waxing lyrical about how great the whole training day had gone and the feedback from the delegates was amazing and how they loved the whole experience. I thought about how wonderful I would be feeling, knowing that it had all been a real success. It completely freed me from the anxiety and concern of the specifics of the situation. Needless to say, because I could separate myself from 'wobbly' specifics, I could once again re-centre. I stayed centred in the feeling and vision of a general overview. And because I was able to come from a steady clear vibrational intention, the day took care of itself, with far more ease and fun than I could ever have tried to imagine or create through a wobble.

So if you have anything that you are focusing on that you really want and the thought of not getting it (such as money to pay your bills) is causing anxiety, take your focus and thought off the specifics of the bill and go general. As you want abundance to flow to you (to pay your bill), intend to notice abundance generally, the beauty of the day around you, the sun shining, the love of friends and/or family etc. You get the idea. Focusing on abundance in a general form will stop you wobbling and will support you in becoming a vibrational match to the abundance all around you and then you have become an attractor to the specifics you want, without having to feel the fear of it.

No shoulds

A big one. Many people live this feeling of 'having to' most of their lives. When an opportunity or new experience comes your way, a likely train of 'should' thought will be 'what will that mean for…?' 'I would love to do that, but I can't because of…' And that's the main reason most people shoot their desires down within seconds of thinking the thought.

Another way of living a 'should' life is when we do things that we absolutely know aren't right for us (whatever right may mean for you). You end up living a life that is limited, a life that isn't really yours and a life that feels heavy with compromise and responsibility. Let me just say here that there are people who thrive on responsibility and what I have just written won't resonate at all and that is perfectly OK. Everything we have written and you have read will contain pockets of 'ahas' and also some teachings that won't resonate at all. And that is exactly as we would want you to respond as you are individual and your filters will be unique. We want you to create what you want and if our teaching supports you to shift something in an area of your life that doesn't feel good and create something different, then we would feel very privileged that we have been able to provide some assistance. If there are areas of your life where you feel good, thrive and everything is as you want it, we would suggest you carry on!

When I look back at my first marriage, I know I turned up that afternoon because the momentum of the wedding had gathered a life of its own and my husband's parents would have been devastated (not to mention my parents' loan). Needless to say, as we have taught in this book, you cannot start a journey from an unhappy place and expect a happy ending. That experience for me was one of a few wake-up calls that I received in an intense decade that followed, when I realised very clearly that to take action from should, a place of rescuing (making it all OK) would only serve to make me and everyone else very unhappy. I started to take ownership of my life. I started to act on my emotional guidance system, only moving towards a decision when it felt good and I felt inspired. I created a life that, apart from when I fall into my human moments, flows with ease, joy, love and abundance.

I now have a phrase that I have ready for when anyone asks me why I am doing whatever it is I am doing. The phrase is **'because I want to'**. I no longer justify what I want or what I do to make it feel easier for others. We are all here to create our own unique lives. I have learned that I'm not here to shape and mould others' lives into creation, but to stay clear within my centre so that I can then come from a useful, supportive and loving vibration to teach others how to mould and shape the best life they can for them, if they choose to.

A life of awesomeness – not mediocrity

Awesomeness sometimes feels a very big word! But why? Is it because you think it is too far away from the life you're living? Do you not even let yourself believe that your life could be the way you want it and the word, awesomeness, could feel far-fetched, even threatening?

And now think about mediocrity – how does that feel? Safe? Solid? OK? Nothing wrong with mediocrity? And again, as I have said earlier in this chapter, if mediocrity feels good for you, then that is OK. I just want to highlight that you are reading a book about change and so I lovingly challenge you that if all aspects of your life felt good to you, you wouldn't have got to the last chapter of this book. You would have stopped reading the book way back. And if you are not satisfied with all aspects of your life, I would again lovingly suggest that you are not living a life of awesomeness, but closer to mediocrity.

During my personal journey on this planet, I have come to understand that I have only this life in this body and that when the time comes to leave the planet, I want to know that my intention was clear – to live a life that felt awesome, whatever that means to me. I can't turn the clock back and re-live difficult moments in a different way. But more importantly, we all came here to live a life of growth, and as we learn and evolve, why can our life not grow and expand with us, if that is what we choose and therefore intend? As we notice things on our planet to appreciate, as we notice how satisfied we are feeling and as we feel joy in the acknowledgement of all of that and more, how awesome does our life feel? It feels amazing, it feels bountiful, everything is in flow and when we live our life on purpose, it feels awesome! And within awesomeness, you cannot find mediocrity. Remember, vibration attracts vibration, like attracts like and so if you are feeling awesome, you are in the vortex of attracting more awesomeness!

I have had some big challenges in my life and curve balls thrown at me out of left field, and as maybe you have done in your life, you have dealt with them and have hopefully moved on as best as you can. But looking back, my life had some elements of being awesome, but because it appeared that I was fire-fighting a lot of the time, struggle was a word that I resonated with and definitely felt my life was mediocre. Interestingly though, I always knew there was more, somewhere and there was a nagging but exciting pull that I could, somehow find the tools to let go of the struggle and live a life of awesomeness, whatever that may be.

And now I can truly say I live a life that I love. I am blessed with my husband and children and the relationship we all have, my wonderful friends who I love to the moon and back, the joy in service with the work I do making a difference to those who want to make a difference. The gift that is the peace and beauty of my home and the wellbeing that abounds in my life and the lives of my family and knowing that there is more joy and abundance to come feels awesome! This is a life that I knew existed somewhere and was certain, taking steps towards it was non-negotiable.

Pam

"Who do you hang out with most of the time
on a daily basis?"
"The sun is always shining."

– David Hawkins

Like Sandra, caring about how I feel towards my goals is important. For most of my life I've believed in something greater than just what I see in front of me, but because I was a 'doer', always on the go, busy, action orientated, I rarely stopped to notice what I wanted or where I was going. I reacted to the stimulus in my environment until I discovered personal development in its many guises.

Doing so brought me 'aha' moment after 'aha' moment, I began to wake up to the possibilities that lay dormant within me, I started to become aware of my thoughts and actions and the reality they created for me based on my emotional vibrations.

Personal development introduced me to core values and belief systems which are driven by emotional states so powerful they create and dominate world views. This was revolutionary and helped me see my limitations were learned and existed because of others' expectations of me since birth. Such expectations caused me to think and act in a certain way in order to get approval, to feel good enough, thus creating experiences that I would call upon over and over in the future to help me measure what my reality and truths were. Becoming aware of this, making small changes such as choosing to think and act differently, over time, created new realities, habits and neural pathways for me.

You already know your values and beliefs come from carer-givers, teachers, peers, culture, friends, media, and generally speaking those you listen to and hang out with on a regular basis. Values and beliefs are emotional, they have polarity, the more we desire something, the more we dislike its opposite.

Polarity binds energy both positive and negative and that affects the cells in our body and the vibration we send out into the Universe and the people it sends to us to 'hang out' with. It's important to think about who you spend time with on a regular basis and how that makes you feel. It's also important to notice if you allow yourself to get caught up in group negativity, moaning and victim-like collaboration, all of which will lower your vibration.

If you want to move forward and attract more of what the Universe has to offer (in the positive), start noticing as of now who you're listening to, hanging out with and the stories you get caught up in. This is an **essential** first step. It doesn't mean you can't still hang out with the people you work or live with, it just means you need to be detached from the emotion that is shared and absorbed. That means listening without attachment. It's a skill, it can be learned.

David Hawkins talks about the Einstein level which is a non-emotional factual level. Hawkins says that thoughts without emotional attachment are just thoughts and will not bring that which we don't want. It's when we add emotion to the thought that we create that which we do or don't want. He goes on to tell us that desire with attachment can lead to dissatisfaction, cravings, addictions and never knowing when enough is enough.

David Hawkins says courage is the place to start in order to make positive change happen and was the emotion I started working on when I decided it was time to step away from fear. Courage has an honesty to it, a reality, it allows you to still feel fear but it's appropriate rather than disproportionate; same with disappointment or any other emotion, it's OK to feel them, you just don't bathe in them. Sadness is real and there are times when it's the required emotion, but when you step into courage there is a confidence and a feeling that you can visit these (negative) emotions, handle and learn from them and then move on.

As Hawkins says, the sun is always shining, we just can't see it because we allow the clouds of guilt, apathy, shame, grief, hopelessness, fear, desire and pride to cloud it day in and day out.

I have a dear friend (I'll call her Anna, who's given me permission to share this story with you), who I love lots, she has battled with cancer for a couple of years now, she is 'trying' everything she can to get better, sometimes she feels OK, sometimes she doesn't, she really tries to be positive but in the face of her challenge she finds it difficult at times. Her energy and vibration yo-yo from day to day and week to week. Early on after her diagnosis she reminded me of her wonderful friend (I'll call her Carol), who I've met once or twice who visits her regularly, the only thing is Carol feels so upset for Anna (as we all do) that she brings a sad and low vibration when she visits and often cries.

This is of course understandable, I've cried quite a few times, but I do it in private. It is natural for us to feel sad if our loved ones are in pain or ill, but as Sandra said earlier in this chapter, it doesn't mean you have to go down to the negative energy state when you are with them. In fact, you don't help the person who is sad by taking their emotion on, you double it. As Anna said, "I live with this problem day in and day out, I know how horrible it is. When I see friends I want to talk about things other than my illness, I want to laugh, I want to think about others." As I said, she told me this early on, I'm grateful she did. It allows me to be me with her and talk about life as it is and not feel guilty because I mistakenly think I should only talk about how awful life is when she and I don't believe it is, although it can appear unfair at times.

We go deep, she has a philosophy degree, we chat about nonsense, we talk about her illness, we talk about other people's illness. We've agreed when she's better we are never going to complain about putting on weight ever again (she has lost a lot of weight and she and I were always complaining about putting on a few pounds here and there), we laugh, we chat about our kids. She's tired when we stop, but it's been a normal conversation, the type we've always had. And when I leave, I leave with good feelings, positive intentions for her improved health, I hold that energy for her and trust she does too.

I'm so glad I learned the lesson of not allowing myself to sink into negativity on automatic pilot many years ago when I was in basic counselling training. I was a big sympathiser, I never saw that sympathy could be a problem, but in counselling training it was pointed out to me that I was too full of sympathy for everyone (there is a time and place for sympathy). I cried with or for people when they shared their sad stories and thought about them over and over, this could be with people I knew and people I didn't.

I would become emotionally distressed by the daily news and people's sad stories, I allowed my emotional energy to be dictated by those around me. I was a sponge and I absorbed others' pain. It hurt. I was a rescuer, I wanted to save others from pain, but I seemed to think it was OK for me to be in pain, but I hated it for others. I was kind to other people (as Sandra mentioned), but I was unkind to me in my thoughts about myself and the way I punished myself by always doing more than was healthy for my body or soul. Perhaps you will recognise this behaviour in yourself.

> *"Don't get through life – grow through it."*
>
> – Muhammad Ali

Through counselling, coaching and energy work I learned to work on myself and stop trying to rescue everyone and start rescuing me. I was shown how to develop empathy instead of sympathy, I learned simple beautiful visualisations that protected my intentions, energy system and positivity from being impacted by others when they were sad. It meant I could still be there for people and hold a loving space for them without allowing myself to soak up their pain, which felt very alien at first. I learned how to step into the vibration of courage and at first it wasn't easy.

It's important I point out right now that protecting your energy doesn't mean you don't care. Of course you do, and it's worth considering that it doesn't help your friend or family member when you feel as upset as they do, all it does is compete with them. It doubles the intensity of their problem and it doubles the negative vibration associated with it, which keeps you both stuck in continuing to stay exactly where you are – both in pain, attracting more of the negative vibration and energetic low.

Since learning new communication skills over the years, I like to listen to my friends and family when they come to me to share a problem. I hold the space sacred for them to share how they feel, I hug them (pre C-19) if they like hugs (I do), I try to soothe and console them from a place of love rather than from a place of rescuer. I send them love, healing and light on a rainbow of colour from my heart to their heart as I was taught in Reiki.

I never tell them to be positive, or chin up or any of those annoying clichés. I aim to be grounded and present, with a respect for where they are coming from, no advice from my world, which is vibrating at a different pace from theirs at that moment.

As an aside, have you noticed how easy it is to tell people what you'd do if you were them? Have you noticed how you don't do what you told them you'd do when you experience the same problem?

Anyway, my intention is to be there for them as they are for me, not try and change what's going on, because I can't, all I can do is feel the love I have for them and support and help if they need me to and I do that by holding the space without thinking I know what is best for them. Because I don't.

So I started this section with who do you hang out with? A way forward? It can be. I repeat for a second time you don't have to drop your vibration down to match those who you hang out with in order to hang out with them. Of course it's much easier to do that than it is to hold on to a positive energy state, but with conscious practice you can be there for people you love who are struggling (some people have a lot to handle in life), whilst maintaining and keeping your positive vibration which may lift them a little just by having you around.

If possible try to get a mix of people to hang out with, see if you can find some upbeat friends or family who see the bright side of life, laugh often and have fun and hang out with them more often, their vibration will rub off on you and yours on them, and before you know it you will be a ball of beautiful high vibration ready to set your goals and manifest your desires your way, with leftover positive energy to support your dear friends and family who may sometimes be struggling.

You can only truly change yourself. Having read this book, beware trying to 'make' your friends or family be positive or see the good side of things when they feel low if this vibration changing idea is new to you, because they might get cross with you (I've been there). You'll feel hurt and might just give up continuing this new positive practice before you've seen the amazing results it can bring into your life.

MYTH DEBUNK: People like us can't change, don't deserve… won't be able to…

MANIFESTATION METHOD: Challenge and change the stories you've accepted as true.

Our wish for you

From reading this book, we hope you're full of good intentions, new dreams and desires and lots of different ideas as to how to manifest them. Our wish for you is that you let this book hold your hand, supporting you to choose the thoughts and emotions that create a life you want.

From all the different techniques we've shared with you, it's a good idea to pick one or two that you enjoy, that you look forward to doing daily, that you'd happily choose to practise again and again. And by doing so, you will see a shift in how you're feeling, thinking, believing and therefore attracting.

Remember we only have a belief because we've practised a thought consistently throughout our lives and never questioned it. We've accepted it as a done deal and therefore feel it is difficult to think something more positive on the same subject. This only appears tricky because it takes focus.

We can *choose* to practise a more empowering thought and the tools in this book and the exercises in the downloadable playsheets www.playsheets.16seconds.co.uk will aid the shift.

The awesomeness of your life is waiting for you. And when someone asks you why you are behaving in a way that supports the joy and expansion of *your* life, answer clearly and unapologetically, *because I want to!*

About the Authors

Pam Lidford

As a young child Pam felt a calling to be of service to others and quickly learned that to truly be of help she needed to work on her own blocks and belief systems. This interest took her on a journey which included investigating training to be a counsellor and therapist, though she eventually trained as a professional coach. Her interests include a love of psychology, neuroscience coaching, people, NLP, TFT, EFT and energy field and somatic work in general.

Before becoming a self-employed coach and trainer in 2006, Pam worked as an adult teacher in London for 15 years. As part of her work, she wrote and delivered the first government funded accredited life coaching course for the general public and later the first BTEC in coaching qualification.

Pam works as a holistic and confidence coach, trains individuals to become professional coaches and mentors and supervises them when qualified. She had the privilege to be awarded Trainer of the Year in 2015 by the APCTC.

She lives with her husband in Hertfordshire, has two children and two grandchildren all of whom mean the world to her. She's been involved in personal development for over 35 years and loves how it's helped her connect to herself, find her purpose and be allowed to share her knowledge with thousands of students and delegates who she feels gratitude and love for.

www.pamlidford.co.uk

Sandra Stocks

Sandra's wake-up call to learn and teach living an authentic and fully realised life happened over 25 years ago after experiencing personal trauma. She found her love of crystals and healing and subsequently attained her Diploma in Vibrational Healing and also qualified as a practitioner in Bach Flower Remedies. She then went on to receive her Distinction in Personal Performance Coaching and also qualified as an NLP practitioner. Sandra uses all her tools to support thousands of people to change their lives to gain personal empowerment, self-belief and a thirst to live and fulfil the potential that they are here to achieve. She also trains young people in authentic leadership and is the lead coach in her group and online programmes. She is now in the process of writing her second book to help people further in finding peace, ease and contentment within the world we live in.

www.sandrastocks.co.uk

Notes

_____

_____

_____

_____

_____

_____

_____

_____

_____

_____

CPSIA information can be obtained
at www.ICGtesting.com
Printed in the USA
LVHW041621010621
689058LV00001B/2

9 781784 529345